PAPER 6

ELEMENTS OF INFORMATION SYSTEMS

First edition 1987
Sixth edition March 1992

ISBN 0 86277 945 6 (previous edition 0 86277 371 7)

British Library Cataloguing-in-Publication Data

A catalogue record for this book
is available from the British Library

Published by

BPP Publishing Limited
Aldine House, Aldine Place
London W12 8AW

Printed in Great Britain by
Ashford Colour Press, Gosport, Hampshire

We are grateful to the Association of Accounting Technicians, the
London Chamber of Commerce and Industry, the Institute of
Chartered Secretaries and Administrators, the Chartered
Association of Certified Accountants and the Chartered Institute
of Management Accountants for permission to reproduce past
examination questions. The suggested solutions have been prepared
by BPP Publishing Limited.

CONTENTS

	Page
Preface	1
Syllabus	2
The examination paper	3
Study guide	8
Flowcharting symbols	14
Test your knowledge: questions	15
Test your knowledge: answers	19
Practice and revision checklist	24
Index to questions and suggested solutions	25
Questions	31
Suggested solutions	53
Test paper: December 1991 examination	165
Test paper: December 1991 examination suggested solutions	169
Further reading	181

PREFACE

The examinations of the Association of Accounting Technicians are a demanding test of students' ability to master the wide range of knowledge and skills required of the modern accountant. The Association's rapid response to the pace of change is shown both in the content of the syllabuses and in the style of examination questions set.

BPP's Practice and Revision Kits are designed to supplement BPP's Study Texts with study material for practice and revision tailored to accommodate recent changes in the style and format of the examination.

The 1992 edition of the Paper 6 Elements of Information Systems kit contains:

- the syllabus and the Association's syllabus guidance notes
- an analysis of recent examination papers, plus summaries of the examiner's comments
- study notes to jog your memory on each area of the syllabus
- a 'test your knowledge' quiz
- a checklist for you to plan your study and keep tabs on your progress
- a question bank divided into topic areas containing:
  - o a total of 19 basic revision questions to warm you up on key techniques before starting the examination standard questions
  - o a total of 62 examination standard questions, most of which come from past examinations, including all examination questions set in at least the last five papers up to and including June 1991
- a full test paper consisting of the December 1991 examination, for you to try out under exam conditions

All questions are provided with full suggested solutions, and there are numerous tutorial notes prepared by BPP. The tutorial notes to past examination questions contain summaries of the examiner's comments where relevant.

If you attempt all the examination standard questions in the kit, together with the test paper, you will have written answers equivalent to nearly 14 examinations. So if you write good answers to all of them, you should be well prepared for anything you meet in the examination itself. Good luck!

BPP Publishing
March 1992

For details of other BPP publications relevant to your studies for this exam, please turn to page 181. Should you wish to send in your comments on this kit please turn to page 182.

SYLLABUS

Aims

To develop an understanding of:

(a) the role of information technology in business, with special reference to the accounting function; and

(b) the methods used to capture, store, process and transmit that information.

Content

20% *Information*

The nature of data and information; the role of information in business; general characteristics of information; methods of information processing from manual to batch, online and interactive methods; general concepts of files, structure, content and organisation.

30% *Hardware*

Input equipment for batch, online and other data capture methods; the central processor unit, structure and function; file hardware and implications for processing methods; output equipment in both hard and soft form; data transmission, modems, multiplexors and local area networks.

30% *Software*

Using and acquiring packages; computer language and utilities; problem definition and flowcharting; programming, principles and good practice.

20% *Organisation and Control*

Procedures for data vet and validations; staff tasks in a DP department; security and controls; standards and documentation.

Questions will not be set on the analysis and design of information systems, which will be examined in Paper 11 - Analysis and Design of Information Systems.

THE EXAMINATION PAPER

Paper format

The examination paper contains seven questions, of which you must answer five. All questions carry equal marks (20). You will be allowed to use flowcharting templates.

Paper content

When it published the pilot paper for this syllabus, the Association also provided an introduction to the syllabus. An extract is reproduced below, because it contains further guidance on the type of questions which are likely to come up in the examination.

'... Candidates should note in particular that the paper is concerned with information systems and the way in which they impact on the accounting technician. Knowledge of programming is not required though the ability to define a logical problem using a flowcharting or decision table technique is necessary, as this type of task may well be carried out by a technician using a high level software tool (eg a query language). An understanding of data which is held in computer files for standard accounting based applications is also needed as is a knowledge of the range of hardware and software tools, which may be used to store, process, retrieve and present the information generated from this data.

Finally the student should appreciate the range of organisation structures in terms of people and equipment with which the technician may come into contact, the need for care in recording and processing of data, the control methods used to ensure good quality control of information and the benefits good information brings to an organisation.'

Paper 6 and Paper 11 (Analysis and Design of Information Systems)

Paper 6 on the Elements of Information Systems leads into Paper 11 (Analysis and Design of Information Systems) in the final examination. Much of the subject area is common to both papers, eg local area networks and standards and documentation. Paper 11, of course, deals with information systems at a more advanced level, but most of what you learn for Paper 6 will recur in your later studies for Paper 11.

It is worth stressing, however, that the syllabus for Paper 6 states that questions will not be set on the Analysis and Design of Information Systems, which will be examined in Paper 11.

However, because the syllabus for Paper 6 leads into the syllabus for Paper 11, it is impossible to divide topic areas in a clear cut way. It is not really possible, for example, to have questions on methods of information processing and the implications of file hardware for processing methods without involving systems flowcharts. This practice and revision kit has therefore covered some topic areas that you might later find examined in Paper 11 because of the lack of a clear cut division between the syllabus for the two papers.

THE EXAMINATION PAPER

Analysis of past papers

A brief analysis of the topics covered by the last eight papers is given below. Each question is cross-referenced to its place in this kit.

December 1991

1 Printers
2 Distributed processing
3 Physical security
4 Files and information
5 Microcomputers
6 Levels of decision-making
7 DP terminology

This paper forms the test paper at the end of the kit, so only an outline of its content is given here.

		Question number in this kit
June 1991		
1	Hardware features of a typical business computer	20
2	EPOS and decision-making	28
3	Data control	33
4	Database management software and maintenance of customer lists	49
5	Operations section of a DP department	61
6	Applications software in an accounts department	50
7	Data storage on disk	70

Examiner's comments

Many candidates ignored the instruction to use a diagram to identify and describe computer hardware (question 1) or ignored the request for 'menu' screens (question 4), presenting instead output screens. This emphasises the need to read the question carefully. Candidates had either thorough or minimal knowledge of EPOS (question 2). Question 5 was the most popular question and those candidates who correctly limited their answers to the operations section generally scored well. Questions 3 and 6, each divided into a number of separate parts, were the questions most frequently attempted last by candidates, many appearing weak in or more parts of each. Question 7, although not popular, was well answered by those candidates who interpreted it properly and did not write about different types of disk.

THE EXAMINATION PAPER

*Question number
in this kit*

December 1990

1	File terms; preparation of flowchart	12
2	Describe mark sensing or OCR or MICR with examples	26
3	Uses of computers in business; questions to ask a supplier	51
4	Output devices	30
5	WIMP operating systems	43
6	Data processing systems vs management information systems	3
7	Data processing standards manual	78

Examiner's comments

Question 1 offered an opportunity to score highly, indeed some candidates obtain full marks, although others were unable to translate their knowledge into an acceptable flow diagram. Question 2 was not well done, very few candidates having a technical understanding of the method chosen. Question 3 was reasonably well done, although in part (b) many candidates phrased the same questions in a number of different ways rather than giving ten discrete relevant questions. Many candidates were not familiar with COM (question 4) or data processing standards (question 7). Some candidates failed to read question 5 properly and wrote a full explanation of the role of the operating system. Question 6 was popular and quite well answered.

June 1990

1	Construct a spreadsheet model	45
2	Data communications terms	35
3	Using a computer bureau to run a payroll application	64
4	Data capture methods	25
5	Draft a sales ledger enquiry screen, and describe the information it contains	11
6	Computer system controls	75
7	Programming terminology	58

Examiner's comments

The question on spreadsheets (question 1) was well done, although some candidates failed to provide examples. In question 4, many candidates wrote about the difference between batch and real-time systems without alluding to data capture methods and in question 2, although similar questions had appeared previously, candidates were unable to define 'asynchronous' or 'protocol'. The question on a payroll bureau (question 3) was poorly answered and many candidates wrote solely about data validation when asked about controls (question 6). Questions 5 and 7 were quite well done, although some candidates confused syntax and logic errors (question 7).

THE EXAMINATION PAPER

Question number in this kit

December 1989

1	Purchase ledger system	14
2	Risks to computer systems	73
3	Hardware devices	21
4	Word processing and desk-top publishing	47
5	Data processing terms	81
6	Batch and real time processing	32
7	DP staff	60

Examiner's comments

Many candidates do not read questions carefully enough. Input devices were described instead of input transactions (question 1) and steps taken to minimise risks were omitted (question 2). Candidates appeared weak on laser printers (question 3), desk-top publishing (question 4) and databases (question 5). Question 6 was a popular question which was generally answered well, as was question 7, although in the former insufficient attention was paid to hardware requirements and in the latter the tasks of data preparation and data control were not clearly distinguished by some.

June 1989

1	Hardware terminology	19
2	Sales order processing system	9
3	Operating systems and 'user friendliness'	42
4	Information terms	4
5	Installation and running costs	65
6	Flow charts etc	55
7	Procedures manual	77

Examiner's comments

Question 1 was not popular; in particular many candidates knew little about 'resolution' or 'interface ports'. Question 2 was generally well answered, although many candidates ignored the relevance of the telephone, and question 6 was also well answered. A major gap in knowledge on systems software was apparent (question 3) and 'query language' (question 4) was not a term with which candidates were familiar. Question 5 produced some good answers, although some candidates wrote about hardware and software costs, despite the question wording. Question 7 was very badly answered, many candidates failing to read the question.

THE EXAMINATION PAPER

		Question number in this kit
December 1988		
1	Good information	2
2	Roles in a DP department	59
3	Simple flowchart description of a batch processing system	15
4	Data processing terms	13
5	Computerised stock control system	8
6	Data capture	24
7	Data management software	48
June 1988		
1	Information distribution	38
2	Spreadsheets	–
3	Computerised fixed assets accounting system	7
4	Software terms	40
5	Integrated systems	52
6	Electronic office, Local Area Networks, Wide Area Networks	36
7	System specification	76

STUDY GUIDE

Using this kit

To warm up, try the *basic revision questions* for each section. Then start the exam-style questions. The more practice you can get in answering exam-style questions, the better prepared you will be for the examination itself. If time is limited, however, remember that a serious attempt at one question is more valuable than cursory attempts at two. Avoid the temptation to 'audit' the answers: try to complete your attempt before checking with our solution. When you have had enough practice to be confident of your grasp of the material, try a few questions under exam conditions, timing yourself against the clock.

To obtain the greatest benefit from the use of this kit you are recommended:

(a) to complete a thorough preparation of each subject before attempting the questions on that subject. Answering questions is a test of what you have learnt and also a means of practising so that you develop a skill in presenting your answers. To attempt them before you are ready is not a fair test of your proficiency and the result may discourage you;

(b) to write your answers in examination conditions without referring to books, manuals or notes. Then refer to the suggested answer in this kit. The suggested answers are only suggestions. They are correct and complete on essentials but there is more than one way of writing an answer;

(c) to follow the subdivisions of the kit so that you use the questions to test what you can do after systematic preparation;

(d) use the practice and revision checklist on page 24 of this kit. Tick off each topic on the checklist as you revise and try questions on it. This will help to ensure that you are on track to complete your revision before the exam.

The questions in this kit are designed to provide a wide coverage of the syllabus. By working through the questions, you should therefore be going over all the topics you ought to learn, and assessing your ability to answer examination-style questions well.

To use this kit properly, you should prepare your own answers to questions first, and then compare the suggested solutions with your own. Look to see how many points of similarity and difference there are between them.

Questions which call for a written answer are difficult to revise with, because it is human nature to be easily bored by writing out lengthy solutions. We would suggest this remedy.

(a) You should attempt a full written solution to one or two questions, in order to gain experience and familiarity with the task of producing solutions within the timescale allowed in the examination itself.

(b) For other questions you should prepare an *answer plan*. This is a list of the points that you would put into your solution, preferably in the order that you would make them.

(c) You should then read our solution and:

   (i)   make a note of points that are new to you and that you think you should learn (eg by underlining certain sentences in the solution for future reference);

   (ii) prepare an answer plan from our own solution, to make sure that you understand that relevance to the question of the points we raise. This useful discipline will ensure that you absorb the points in solutions more thoroughly.

Notes on specific areas of the syllabus

The notes below are to help you revise material you should know already. They are not a substitute for your study text.

Information

This section of the syllabus requires you to consider information and information systems from a general point of view. It is much easier to learn facts about hardware and software than it is the more abstract topics of data and information.

Going back to first principles, you are required to be aware of data and information, the role of information in business and the general characteristics of information. Try and apply these ideas to your work environment.

A distinction sometimes made is that information is data that has been processed to make it meaningful and useful to the person who receiving it. Whether an item of fact is data or information depends to a degree on the position of the recipient. What is information to a clerk may be only data to a manager. For example, basic payroll details may be used to prepare a report on a monthly basis for the personnel department. This is useful information to them as they use the payroll it at the end of every year to prepare forms for tax purposes. The contents of the report may also be used in the accounts department as data for the monthly management accounting information presented to senior management.

Try Q3 *Data processing systems and MIS*

The above example might give us a hint as to why information is used in any organisation. Information is needed to plan and control an enterprise, but its use alters at different layers of management. The payroll provides management at *operational* level with the information that lets them know that wages and related tax deductions have been calculated correctly. Should there be any enquiries, it is an important document for reference. At *tactical* (middle management) level this material would be used to document wage trends in the organisation as a whole, comparison with budget, and investigation of differences. At *strategic* level, long term information provided by the payroll would be useful in planning the organisation's future development.

So we have seen that different levels of management have different information needs, but all information must display certain basic qualities. Revise your study text for the qualities of good information.

Try Q2 *Information* and Q4 *Information terms*

Having revised data and information, we can descend into the nitty gritty of data processing. We know that data is processed information, but the data can be processed in a number of different ways. The basic model for any processing system is as follows.

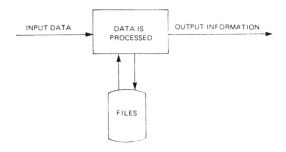

In any data and information processing system, whether manual or computerised transaction data can be input and processed:

- immediately as it arises (on demand); or
- in a group (or batch), built up over a period of time.

A variant on demand processing is *real-time* processing which occurs when not only does processing occur immediately but the results of the processing are made known to the operator. An airline reservation system is a prime example of real-time processing.

Finally, data are collected and held in files. The processing operation may involve using information that is held in a file, or altering a file in some way. There are many kinds of files for example:

- transaction files, contain data to be input and processed in a batch processing system;
- master-files contain the results of processed data and some standing details;
- reference files;
- database files contain data that can be used in a number of different ways.

Files are a collection of records: a record is a definable unit of information (eg purchase ledger transaction), and is made out of fields (eg supplier name).

With these concepts in mind, the examiner might ask you to apply them to an accounting system (eg payroll). Do not be intimidated. These are the systems you probably use in your day-to-day working environment. You might be required to indicate fields on a payroll file, or the processing sequence of a stock file. If your job involves you with one of these applications, you can use that as a starting point for your answer.

There is a large number of questions on files and processing. Try Q13 *Processing terms*, and then some of Q7 to Q12.

Hardware

This section is where we start getting to the detail of computerised data processing: the technology in information technology as it were. You are simply required to know the nuts and bolts of computing. A good question to test your knowledge is Q19 *Hardware terminology* which probes your ability to decode some of the jargon that surrounds computing.

A few revision points

(1) *Input*

Try and think of the variety of input methods you come across in daily life:

- a cheque is an example of MICR (magnetic ink character recognition)
- the bar-codes used at a supermarket checkout (a type of optical mark reading)
- the magnetic stripe used in an ATM (cashpoint) card

All these are example of *direct data entry*. The information is captured directly by the computer. There is no need for the data to be transcribed into a computer-sensible form. On the other hand, if you are presented with a pile of invoices, each of which has to be coded, and the details have to be keyed in to a tape or diskette, this is an example of transcription.

One of the common forms of data input in office life is direct keyboard entry. Input can be seen on a VDU screen. Keyboard and VDU are essential prerequisites for interactive processing. Try Q25 *Data entry* and Q26 *Direct document reading*.

(2) *Central processor unit*

You need to keep a number of factors in mind here.

●   The CPU is a collection of electrical circuits, switched ON or OFF, a fact that is important for programming, as these states are represented by the binary digits (bits) 1 and 0; a character (eg a letter or number) is often represented by 8 bits (a byte).

●   The CPU is organised into a control unit directing the sequence of operations and implementing coded instructions, the arithmetic and logic unit performing calculations and comparisons, and internal store (immediate access store, main memory) which holds input data and programs for use by the ALU and CPU.

●   The difference between RAM and ROM memory is that RAM is alterable, whereas ROM is normally fixed.

●   Data can travel in series (one bit at a time) or in parallel (eight bits at a time); data travels in parallel inside the CPU (along buses), but may need converting to serial form by a serial interface.

●   The power of a computer is often determined by the size of its main memory and the speed with which instructions are executed.

●   Remember to revise the difference between mainframe, mini and microcomputer.

(3) *Backing store*

Backing store is where data and program *files* are stored before input for processing to the CPU. Data and programs from backing store are transferred to the CPU's internal store. Types of backing store hardware include:

●   magnetic tape;
●   magnetic disk;
●   optical disk.

The choice of hardware for backing store determines the type of processing that can be achieved.

Tape is run past a read/write head. Data held on tape can only be accessed in a particular sequence. In a disk system, it is possible to access data directly. What implications do you think this has for file organisation?

Try Q31 *Disks and tapes* and Q32 *Batch and real-time processing.*

(4) *Output*

There is little you need worry about here, provided you have done your learning properly. So, revise your knowledge on printers, COM and so forth. Remember that VDU screen display is also a form of output.

Try Q30 *Computer output.*

(5) *Data transmission*

Some organisations like computers and peripheral equipment to communicate with each other over a distance. Communications can be over a telecommunications link, in which case special equipment (eg modems) may be needed, as long as telecommunications links require data to be sent in analog rather than digital format. (Revise your text for the difference between analog and digital.) Try Q35 *Data communication terms.*

Data transmission enables:

● input to be made at different sites to where processing occurs;
● processing to be distributed over central sites, but with files held in one place;
● direct communication between computers and other devices.

Revise the difference between LANs and WANs. Try Q36 *Networks* and Q39 *IT terms.*

Software

Software comprises computer programs. A program is a set of instructions telling a computer to execute a particular task, or tasks. Software has many uses.

1   Operating systems (OS) software controls the resources within a data processing installation. Try Q42 *Operating system.*

2   Programming tools are software that enable other software to be written.

3   Application software is software designed to do a particular task:

● utilities perform functions (eg print, sort) required by other programs;

● some applications packages are sets of programs which can be purchased as they are designed to integrate a number of processing operations in one (eg sales ledger package);

● general purpose applications packages provide a set of facilities to the user (eg a spreadsheet modelling).

There are a number of questions on this topic. Try Q41 *Basic revision question: packages.* For details of particular types of package try Q45 *Spreadsheet facilities,* Q47 *Word processing and desk-top publishing* and Q48 *Data management software.*

You will recall (if you don't you certainly should) that a computer deals with information in the form of binary digits representing the ON/OFF states of its electrical circuits. Any instructions for the computer must be expressed in binary digits (called machine code). However, this is very time consuming to write. *Assembly languages* were developed as abbreviations of machine code, yet still reflect the physical activity of the computer. *High level languages* were later developed dispensing with binary notation, and on the whole only reflect the logic of the processing rather than the way it is carried out physically.

All programs written in a programming language must be translated into machine code. A program written in a programming language is called source code; its machine code equivalent is called an object code. Do you remember the difference between compilers and interpreters? Try Q58 *Terminology in programming.*

Programs are written in a language to solve a problem or execute an instruction. The logic of the problem has to be defined, and two methods used are flowcharts and decision tables. There are a number of questions available for practice. At least, try Q55 *Logical representation.*

Organisation and control

Security and controls

Controls is a very generalised area of the syllabus. It includes the detail of data validation procedures eg the use of check digits, range checks etc. These you must simply learn. Also covered are more general issues such as controls over the environment in which a computer system operates. Your only option is to apply your technical knowledge with a certain amount of common sense. Try and list some dangers to computer systems. You will find that you can identify dangers to hardware of a physical nature (eg fire, floods), the effects of which can be mitigated by proper planning and backup procedures. Other threats to computer systems and the data held on them are those caused by human intervention, whether they be accidental or malicious. Stretch your imagination and think of ways in which on the one hand:

(1) you could wreak havoc on your organisation's computer systems; and on the other

(2) you could provide security measures against the threats you have identified in (1).

Try Q72 *Physical security*, Q73 *Minimise risks*, and Q75 *Ten controls.*

Staff roles

Staff roles are examined regularly. If your employer runs a DP department why not ask how it is run? A diagram is provided below to jog your memory.

Organisation chart for a DP department

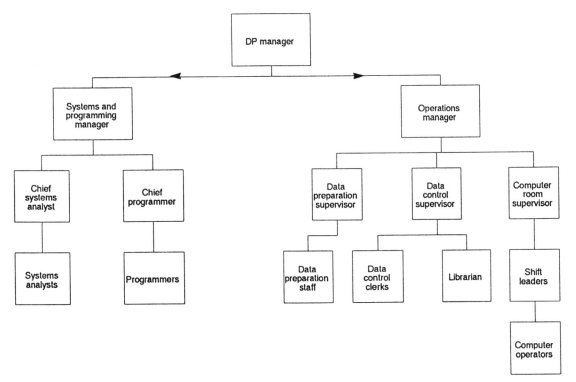

FLOWCHARTING SYMBOLS

In the event that you are asked in an examination question to describe the meaning of a flowchart or to use a flowchart, you need to know about the variety of flowcharting symbols used.

NCC symbols

The flowcharting symbols recommended by the National Computing Centre Ltd are deliberately restricted in number, to avoid unnecessary confusion. These symbols are:

Symbol	Meaning
	Any type of operation
	Computer backing storage files (magnetic disk, tape, diskette, etc)
	Input or output
	Connector, to show continuity of the chart's flow where it is not possible to join up symbols with a flowline
	Start or end symbol
	Decision symbol, used in program flowcharts

TEST YOUR KNOWLEDGE: QUESTIONS

Try the following short questions on each major area of the syllabus. They will help to pinpoint any important gaps in your knowledge, and consolidate what you already know. Check your answer against those shown on the following pages.

1. What would you see as the qualities of good information?

2. Define a computer.

3. What are the *six* basic components of a computer?

4. Define the following terms:

    (a) hardware;
    (b) software.

5. Distinguish between the terms *data capture* and *data collection*.

6. What are the main factors likely to influence a company's choice of output equipment and media?

7. What are the main factors to be considered when selecting a data transmission system?

8. Name *three* different types of file typically found within a processing system.

9. The *hit rate* is an important consideration when determining the choice of external storage media. Define *hit rate*.

10. Name the *four* main components of a magnetic tape unit.

11. Name the *two* methods of file organisation available with tape files.

12. What are the *three* elements of access time when using an exchangeable disk pack file?

13. Name the *four* methods of file organisation available with disk files.

14. What is the name given to the smallest addressable part of a disk, being the unit of input and output in disk systems?

15. Name the *three* basic types of processing methods used in computer systems.

16. Name any *five* editing checks typically found within a data validation program.

17. Define a database.

18. What do these letters stand for:

    (a) RJE?
    (b) OCR?
    (c) COM?
    (d) MODEM?

19. Name the *three* major functions of an operating system.

20. Name any *four* of the main types of *utility software* (service programs) available.

21. What is the name given to the program used to convert from source to object program in relation to:

    (a) high level languages?
    (b) low level languages?

22. Briefly identify *five* of the main advantages of using high level languages.

23. What are the names given to the *four* quadrants in the standard format for a limited entry decision table?

24. What are the *five* main advantages of using decision tables?

25. Name any of the *five* main duties of the computer librarian.

26. What should be the *five* main features in a computer run chart relating to the batch processing of transactional data?

27. Name *four* of the services which will typically be available from a computer bureau.

28. Using the modulus 11 system, what would be the check digit for the basic code number 4891?

29. What type of errors are check digits designed to detect?

Multiple choice

30. The arithmetic and logic unit is able to determine:

    A if the value of A is equal to, less than or greater than the value of B;
    B whether a value is positive or negative;
    C whether a value is zero;
    D all of the above.

31. Which of the following options is correct? Direct access storage media comprise(s) *only*

    A magnetic tape;
    B magnetic disks;
    C optical disks;
    D B and C.

32. When records on a magnetic disk are organised indexed-sequentially, the most efficient method of access is:

    A selective sequential;
    B serial;
    C sequential;
    D random.

33. The central processing unit (CPU) is made up of:

    A   the arithmetic and logic units and output devices;
    B   the main store, the control unit and the arithmetic and logic unit;
    C   input devices, output devices and backing store;
    D   all of the above.

34. Which of the following terms or expressions never refers to a disk file?

    A   file generation technique;
    B   write permit ring;
    C   cylinders;
    D   buckets.

35. A file is defined as:

    A   a collection of related records;
    B   a collection of related fields;
    C   a collection of related characters;
    D   all of the above.

36. Selective-sequential access is associated *only* with:

    A   a disk file;
    B   a serial access file;
    C   a magnetic tape file;
    D   disk files and tape files.

37. A check digit is:

    A   an alpha or numeric character associated with a code or key;
    B   Modulus 11;
    C   a random number;
    D   a type of password.

38. Which of the following validation tests would be the most appropriate to identify missing input records?

    A   sequence test and/or record count;
    B   a range and/or limit test;
    C   a format test;
    D   a check digit.

39. An object program is:

    A   produced by a compiler;
    B   a tested program;
    C   a program written in a low level language;
    D   a program written in a high level language.

40. Input validation should be done:

   A   before verification;
   B   before batching of documents;
   C   after data conversion but before update;
   D   after update but before distribution of output.

41. Which of the following is false?

   A   decision tables can be used for fact recording and analysis;
   B   distributed processing is the function of data control;
   C   branching, looping and logic testing are programming techniques;
   D   graph plotters are computer output devices.

42. One of the following is an example of management information rather than routine operating information:

   A   a goods received note;
   B   a customer statement;
   C   a despatch note;
   D   an expenditure variance analysis report.

43. Which of the following are true?

   A   conversational computing uses voice input;
   B   COBOL is a low-level language;
   C   a compiler is an item of software;
   D   a program specification is usually written by a programmer.

44. The proportion of records accessed on a master file during update is known as:

   A   file organisation;
   B   hit rate;
   C   transfer rate;
   D   packing density.

TEST YOUR KNOWLEDGE: ANSWERS

1. Information should be communicated:

   (a) by an appropriate communication channel;

   (b) with as little ambiguity or misunderstanding as possible;

   (c) with clarity;

   (d) to the right people;

   (e) at the right time;

   (f) with sufficient confidence in its accuracy;

   (g) it must also be comprehensive, and should be directed towards the goals of the company as a whole;

   (h) it must also be provided at a cost which is less than the value of the benefits it provides.

2. Any device capable of accepting data automatically, applying a sequence of processes to the data, and supplying the results of these processes.

3. (a) Input;

   (b) external storage;

   (c) internal storage;

   (d) ALU;

   (e) control unit;

   (f) output.

4. (a) Hardware may be simply defined as the physical and electromechanical components of a computer system.

   (b) Software may be defined as the control systems, programs and other support services required to operate the computer hardware.

5. Data capture is usually taken to mean the capture of data in machine sensible form at its source, as opposed to data collection, which is the process of collecting the data (in any form) and converting it into machine sensible form for input to the computer.

6. (a) The suitability of the application;

   (b) the speed at which the output is required;

   (c) whether a printed version is required;

   (d) the volume of information;

   (e) the cost of the method chosen as compared with the benefits to be derived.

TEST YOUR KNOWLEDGE: ANSWERS

7. (a) The speed of transmission required;

    (b) volume of data to be processed;

    (c) whether data transmission will be one way or two way;

    (d) accuracy and reliability required;

    (e) costs of each type of data transmission method;

    (f) whether or not data should be transmitted direct to the computer (on-line).

8. (a) Transaction files;

    (b) reference files;

    (c) master files.

9. The percentage of master file records which, on average, will be processed during a routine update.

10. (a) 2 reel holders;

    (b) a tape drive mechanism;

    (c) read, write and erase heads;

    (d) vacuum chambers.

11. (a) Serial;

    (b) sequential.

12. (a) Seek time;

    (b) rotational delay;

    (c) data transfer time.

13. (a) Serial;

    (b) sequential;

    (c) indexed sequential;

    (d) random.

14. A sector (block or bucket).

15. (a) Batch processing of all data.

    (b) Demand processing for file interrogation followed by subsequent batch processing for updating of files at off-peak times.

    (c) Demand processing of all data and immediate file update (real time processing).

TEST YOUR KNOWLEDGE: ANSWERS

16. Any five from:

    (a) range checks;

    (b) limit checks;

    (c) existence check;

    (d) format check;

    (e) combination check;

    (f) sequence check;

    (g) completeness check;

    (h) field comparison and cross check;

    (i) check digit verification.

17. A database is a collection of data so organised that data items in it can be accessed through related data items, but without duplicating these items.

18. (a) Remote job entry;

    (b) optical character recognition;

    (c) computer originated microform (or computer output in microform);

    (d) modulator/demodulator.

19. (a) Operator/computer communication;

    (b) control of peripheral devices;

    (c) control of all software/multiprogramming.

20. Any four from:

    (a) file conversion;

    (b) file copying (dumping);

    (c) memory dumping;

    (d) file reorganisation;

    (e) file maintenance;

    (f) debugging;

    (g) sorting/merging;

    (h) housekeeping routine;

21. (a) Compiler program;

    (b) assembler program.

22. (a) It is much faster to code programs;

    (b) error correction and testing of programs is easier;

    (c) it is easier for persons other than the author to understand the program;

    (d) programs can be written by persons not possessing a detailed knowledge of computers (ie problem oriented);

    (e) they are more machine independent.

23. (a) Condition stub;

    (b) condition entry;

    (c) action stub;

    (d) action entry.

24. (a) It is possible to check that all combinations have been considered;

    (b) they show a cause and effect relationship;

    (c) it is easy to trace from actions to conditions;

    (d) they are easy to understand and copy as they use a standard format;

    (e) alternatives can be grouped to facilitate analysis.

25. Any five from:

    (a) controlling the issue and return of files;

    (b) ensuring that access to files is restricted to authorised personnel;

    (c) maintaining external file labels;

    (d) allocating a unique identification number to each file and ensuring that this is checked before use;

    (e) ensuring that files containing out of date or corrupt information cannot be confused with live files;

    (f) attempting to ensure that files containing data for retention are not sent to the computer room until the retention period is over;

    (g) ensuring that duplicate files are properly maintained;

    (h) ensuring that there are enough physical files in stock to satisfy all user needs.

TEST YOUR KNOWLEDGE: ANSWERS

26. (a) Input;

    (b) validate;

    (c) sort;

    (d) update;

    (e) output.

27. Any four from:

    (a) data preparation;

    (b) hiring computer time;

    (c) do-it-yourself;

    (d) consultancy;

    (e) software;

    (f) time sharing/RJE;

    (g) turnkey operation.

28. Check digit would be 7.

29. Transposition and transcription errors.

Multiple choice

Question	Answer	Question	Answer
30	D	38	A
31	D	39	A
32	A	40	C
33	B	41	B
34	B	42	D
35	A	43	C
36	A	44	B
37	A		

PRACTICE AND REVISION CHECKLIST

This page is designed to help you chart your progress through this Practice and Revision Kit and thus through the Association's syllabus. By this stage you should have worked through the Study Text, including the illustrative questions at the back of it. You can now tick off each topic as you revise and try questions on it, either of the basic revision type or of the full examination type. Insert the question numbers and the dates you complete them in the relevant boxes. You will thus ensure that you are on track to complete your revision before the exam.

The checklist is arranged in topic order, and follows the content of this Practice and Revision Kit, the corresponding BPP Study Text and the Association's syllabus.

	Revision of study text chapter(s)	*Basic revision questions in kit*	*Examination style questions*
	Ch No/Date Comp	Ques No/Date Comp	Ques No/Date Comp
Information			
Nature, role and characteristics			
Files			
Processing methods			
Hardware			
The computer			
Input and output			
Storage and processing			
Data transmission			
Software			
Types of software			
Application packages			
Problem definition			
Languages and programming			
Organisation and control			
Staffing			
Security and control			
DP standards			

Test paper

Date completed

INDEX TO QUESTIONS AND SUGGESTED SOLUTIONS

As far as possible, questions have been listed under the appropriate headings from the syllabus. But some questions span more than one area of the syllabus: where this is the case, a question has been placed under the heading which is most relevant to its content. The suggested solutions have been designed as aids to learning: you will not have the time to reproduce such detail in the examination itself.

		Question	*Suggested solution*
INFORMATION			
Nature, role and characteristics			
1	*Basic revision question: company information systems*	31	53
2	Information (12/88)	31	53
3	Data processing systems and MIS (12/90)	31	54
4	Information terms (6/89)	31	56
File organisation			
5	*Basic revision question: file type*	31	57
6	*Basic revision question: payroll master file*	32	57
7	Fixed assets accounting system (6/88)	32	58
8	Stock control system (12/88)	32	59
9	Sales order processing system (6/89)	33	61
10	Sales ledger system (6/87)	33	62
Processing methods			
11	Sales ledger enquiry screen (6/90)	33	63
12	File processing terms and diagram (12/90)	34	65
13	Processing terms (12/88)	34	67
14	Purchase ledger system (12/89)	34	69
15	Batch processing flowchart (12/88)	34	70
16	*Basic revision question: batch and interactive processing*	35	73
HARDWARE			
General hardware questions			
17	*Basic revision question: computer model*	35	74
18	*Basic revision question: central processing unit*	36	75
19	Hardware terminology (6/89)	36	77
20	Hardware features (6/91)	36	78
21	Hardware devices (12/89)	36	79
Input and output			
22	*Basic revision question: input and output*	36	82
23	*Basic revision question: data capture*	37	83
24	Data capture (12/88)	37	83
25	Data entry (6/90)	37	84
26	Direct document reading (12/90)	37	85
27	*Basic revision question: point of sale terminals*	37	88

INDEX TO QUESTIONS AND SUGGESTED SOLUTIONS

		Question	Suggested solution
28	EPOS (6/91)	37	89
29	*Basic revision question: printers*	38	90
30	Computer output (12/90)	38	90

Storage and processing

31	Disks and tapes	38	93
32	Batch and real-time processing (12/89)	38	94
33	Data storage on disk (6/91)	38	95

Data transmission

34	*Basic revision question: telecommunications terms*	39	96
35	Data communication terms (6/90)	39	97
36	Networks (6/88)	39	98
37	XAB Ltd (12/87)	39	100
38	MM Enterprises (6/88)	39	101
39	IT terms	40	103

SOFTWARE

Types of software

40	Software terminology (6/88)	40	103
41	*Basic revision question: packages*	40	105
42	Operating systems (6/89)	40	106
43	WIMP operating system (12/90)	40	107

Application packages

44	*Basic revision question: spreadsheets*	41	108
45	Spreadsheet facilities (6/90)	41	110
46	*Basic revision question: word processor*	41	112
47	Word processing and desk-top publishing (12/89)	41	113
48	Data management software (12/88)	41	114
49	Database management (6/91)	41	115
50	Software applications (6/91)	42	117
51	Business systems (12/90)	42	118
52	Integrated systems: nominal ledger (6/88)	42	120

Problem definition and flowcharting

53	Decision table (6/86)	42	121
54	Flowchart	43	124
55	Logical representation (6/89)	43	125

INDEX TO QUESTIONS AND SUGGESTED SOLUTIONS

		Question	*Suggested solution*
Languages and programming			
56	*Basic revision question: languages*	43	126
57	*Basic revision question: structured techniques*	44	126
58	Terminology in programming (6/90)	44	127
ORGANISATION AND CONTROL			
Staff tasks in a DP department; DP resources			
59	DP department (12/88)	44	129
60	Staff roles (12/89)	44	130
61	Data processing staff (6/91)	45	133
62	*Basic revision question: computer bureau*	45	136
63	Computerised payroll (12/86)	45	137
64	Payroll and bureau (6/90)	45	139
65	Installation and running costs (6/89)	45	140
66	Assessing a DP project (6/87)	45	141
Security and control			
67	*Basic revision question: risks and controls*	46	142
68	Controls over input and stored data	46	142
69	Batch control system (12/87)	46	145
70	Data control (6/91)	46	145
71	*Basic revision question: security*	47	147
72	Physical security (12/86)	47	148
73	Minimise risks (12/89)	47	149
74	Internal control in a DP system	47	150
75	Ten controls (6/90)	47	153
Standards and documentation			
76	System specification (6/88)	48	155
77	Procedures manual (6/89)	48	156
78	Data processing standards manual (12/90)	48	157
GENERAL TERMINOLOGY QUESTIONS			
79	DP terms	48	159
80	Explain and illustrate	48	160
81	Sundry terms (12/89)	49	161

QUESTIONS

1 BASIC REVISION QUESTION: COMPANY INFORMATION SYSTEMS (10 marks)

Identify *five* typical weaknesses in company information systems.

2 INFORMATION (20 marks)   12/88

Information systems aim to provide useful information to aid the decision making process. To meet this aim the information produced should be error free and be of good quality.

(a) Identify and explain *four* different points of the data processing cycle at which errors may occur in the production of information from a computerised system.   (8 marks)

(b) State *eight* characteristics of good quality information and explain each one in a few words.   (12 marks)

3 DATA PROCESSING SYSTEMS AND MIS (20 marks)   12/90

Most organisations have *data processing systems* but few as yet have *management information systems*.

(a) Explain what is meant by these two terms and clarify the difference between them.   (10 marks)

(b) Give *two* examples of management decisions that might be made from a management information system and identify the type of supporting information that the system would provide in these cases.   (10 marks)

4 INFORMATION TERMS (20 marks)   6/89

Explain the following terms as they are used in a data processing context, using examples to illustrate your answer.

(a) Raw data   (4 marks)
(b) Exception report   (4 marks)
(c) Strategic information   (4 marks)
(d) Graphical information   (4 marks)
(e) Query language   (4 marks)

5 BASIC REVISION QUESTION: FILE TYPE (10 marks)

You are required to state the entries to be shown in the chart below for (i), (ii), (iii), (iv) and (v).

Nature of processing	Hit rate	Method of organisation	Type of file
Real-time	Low	Random	Disk
Batch	High (ii)	(i) Random	Tape (iii)
Combination of real time and batch	Sometimes high Sometimes low*	(iv)	(v)

* eg where for weekly update the hit rate is high and for enquiries during the week the hit rate is low.

6 BASIC REVISION QUESTION: PAYROLL MASTER FILE (10 marks)

What might be the records, record fields and key record field in a payroll master file?

7 FIXED ASSETS ACCOUNTING SYSTEM (20 marks)   6/88

BMP plc has computerised its fixed assets accounting system.

Required

(a) Name *eight* data fields that you would expect to find in each master record in the assets file.   (4 marks)

(b) Identify and explain the effects of *four* different transactions used to update the file.
                                                                                        (8 marks)

(c) Suggest *two* different outputs from the system indicating in simple layout form, the information that would be presented.   (8 marks)

8 STOCK CONTROL SYSTEM (20 marks)   12/88

Carspares Ltd is a company specialising in supply of car parts to the trade. They stock over 5,000 different items and have a computerised Stock Control System.

(a) List *ten* fields you would expect to find on each stock record and explain their purpose.
                                                                                        (10 marks)

(b) Identify *four* transactions you would expect to occur regularly to update this file.
                                                                                        (4 marks)

(c) Specify *two* screen or paper based reports that the system might produce, and briefly explain their purpose.   (6 marks)

9   SALES ORDER PROCESSING SYSTEM (20 marks)   6/89

Pharmachem plc has a computerised *sales order processing system* where chemists telephone orders to a central team who enter details at a computer terminal, in order that the system can generate delivery notes and invoice documents to go with the goods.

(a)   Explain how such a system would work and identify the data that would be required over the telephone.   (10 marks)

(b)   List the fields that you would expect to be held on the customer file.   (4 marks)

(c)   Explain *two* ways in which this system could reduce the danger of bad debts. (6 marks)

10   SALES LEDGER SYSTEM (20 marks)   6/87

All data processing systems consist of inputs, processes (including storage and retrieval) and outputs.

For a sales ledger system list and briefly describe:

(a)   typical inputs;   (4 marks)
(b)   data stored;   (8 marks)
(c)   other processes carried put;   (4 marks)
(d)   typical outputs.   (4 marks)

11   SALES LEDGER ENQUIRY SCREEN   (20 marks)   6/90

Data processing is often explained using the model given below.

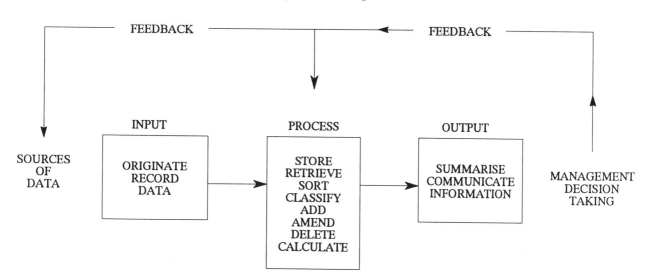

A sales ledger enquiry is a typical output from a data processing system.

(a)   Draft a sample sales ledger enquiry screen.   (8 marks)

(b) List the data fields which must be stored and retrieved to provide the basis of this output screen. (6 marks)

(c) Specify *two* decisions which this report will influence and give reasons for your choice. (4 marks)

12 FILE PROCESSING TERMS AND DIAGRAM (20 marks) 12/90

(a) Briefly explain the following data processing terms:

File
Record
Field
Key
Sort (10 marks)

(b) Draw a flow diagram of a data input and update process which shows how these terms are used in practice. (10 marks)

13 PROCESSING TERMS (20 marks) 12/88

Explain using simple examples the following data processing terms.

(a) Batch processing (5 marks)
(b) On-line processing (5 marks)
(c) Distributed data processing (5 marks)
(d) Timesharing (5 marks)

14 PURCHASE LEDGER SYSTEM (20 marks) 12/89

All Data Processing systems consist of inputs, processes (including storage and retrieval) and outputs. For a Purchase Ledger system list and briefly describe:

(a) *three* typical input transactions. (6 marks)

(b) *eight* data fields which would be stored on the Master file. (4 marks)

(c) *four* processes other than storage/retrieval which would be carried out. (4 marks)

(d) *two* typical outputs and the information they provide. (6 marks)

15 BATCH PROCESSING FLOWCHART (20 marks) 12/88

Describe with the aid of a flowchart, a batch processing system where a large number of transactions are input, validated, sorted, matched and updated against a master file which is held in ascending sequence on magnetic tape. The flowchart should show where error listings would be produced to indicate both input and update errors.

16 BASIC REVISION QUESTION: BATCH AND INTERACTIVE PROCESSING (16 marks)

(a) Describe the characteristics of batch and interactive processing for a computer-based information system. (4 marks)

(b) Compare and contrast these two alternative processing systems, batch and interactive, with respect to:

    (i)   entry of data;
    (ii)   validation of input;
    (iii) correction of errors;
    (iv) order of transactions;
    (v)   back-up facilities for master file;
    (vi) back-up facilities for transactions. (12 marks)

17 BASIC REVISION QUESTION: COMPUTER MODEL (10 marks)

A common analogy used to describe a computer is displayed below.

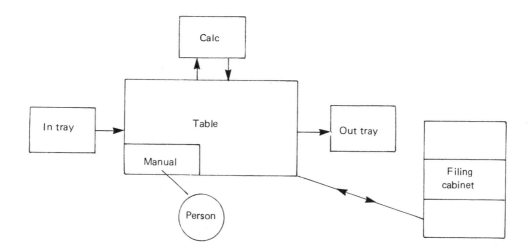

Required

In a typical small business microcomputer system identify the alternative forms available and explain the role of the equivalent devices to:

(a) the in-tray; (2 marks)
(b) the out-tray; (2 marks)
(c) the filing cabinet; (2 marks)
(d) the table; (2 marks)
(e) the procedures manual. (2 marks)

18   BASIC REVISION QUESTION: CENTRAL PROCESSING UNIT

   (a)   With the aid of a diagram show the relationship between the major components of a computer system *and* explain the function and operation of the central processing unit.

   (b)   Describe the binary system of counting.

   (c)   Why does the central processing unit of a computer use binary as a language?

   (d)   With specific reference to the microcomputer, compare and contrast RAM and ROM.

19   HARDWARE TERMINOLOGY   (20 marks)   6/89

The specification of a typical business microcomputer is as follows.

Intel 8088 16 bit processor
256k bytes RAM
20mb hard disc storage
360kb floppy disc storage
800 x 400 pixel high resolution graphics
2 x RS232 asynchronous/synchronous ports
1 Parallel/IEE port

Explain the meaning and purpose of each of these items and comment on the specification given (eg 20mb).

20   HARDWARE FEATURES   (20 marks)   6/91

Identify and describe the hardware features of a typical business computer with which you are familiar. Ensure that you cover the means of input, output, backing storage and memory, and identify the processor used and the method of hard copy production. (Use a diagram to illustrate your answer.)

21   HARDWARE DEVICES   (20 marks)   12/89

Describe the function and potential use of *four* of the following modern hardware devices.

   (a)   Mouse.
   (b)   Laser printer.
   (c)   Winchester disk drive.
   (d)   Hi-resolution monitor.
   (e)   Magnetic stripe reader.

22   BASIC REVISION QUESTION: INPUT AND OUTPUT   (10 marks)

Describe the following components of a typical microcomputer as used by a small business.

   (a)   Input/output.   (5 marks)
   (b)   Data storage.   (5 marks)

23 BASIC REVISION QUESTION: DATA CAPTURE (12 marks)

Explain the terms *direct document reading, turnround documents*, and *on-line data entry* and give an illustration of each of these methods of data capture.

24 DATA CAPTURE (20 marks)   12/88

Identify *four* significantly different approaches to capturing data on to a computer and explain how they differ in terms of speed and human/computer activity.

25 DATA ENTRY (20 marks)   6/90

Batch processing systems typically utilise *key to disk* as a data capture method whereas real time systems normally use *visual display units* for data entry.

Explain the features of these two data capture methods by using appropriate examples which demonstrate their fit with the different processing methods identified.

26 DIRECT DOCUMENT READING (20 marks)   12/90

There are a number of ways of capturing data directly into a computer through the use of machine readable documents. These include *mark sensing*, *optical character recognition* and *magnetic ink character recognition*.

Describe in some detail how *one* of these methods works and give an account of a particular application area where it would be used.

27 BASIC REVISION QUESTION: POINT OF SALE TERMINALS (12 marks)

Cans & Co is a small wholesale grocery company offering discount prices to cash and carry customers. The company has recently installed Point of Sale terminals linked to a computer in the warehouse, to improve their business efficiency.

(a) List *four* benefits Cans & Co hopes to achieve by the installation of this equipment.
(8 marks)
(b) Identify the main files that will need to be maintained on the computer to achieve these benefits.   (4 marks)

28 EPOS (20 marks)   6/91

EPOS (electronic point of sale) systems provide a powerful aid to decision making in retail organisations.

(a) Explain how EPOS systems work in practice.   (8 marks)

(b) Provide *four* examples of the information they provide, explaining in each case the decision that is being supported.   (12 marks)

29 BASIC REVISION QUESTION: PRINTERS (12 marks)

Briefly describe the following types of printer mechanism and explain when each would be the preferred choice.

(a) Daisy wheel
(b) Matrix
(c) Thermal

30 COMPUTER OUTPUT (20 marks)   12/90

A wide range of computer output devices is now available to the user.

Explain the features of the following approaches to computer output and give an example of possible use.

(a) Computer output on microform   (5 marks)
(b) Graph plotter   (5 marks)
(c) High resolution monitor   (5 marks)
(d) Daisy wheel printer   (5 marks)

31 DISKS AND TAPES (20 marks)

(a) Describe the way in which records are organised, accessed and updated on:

    (i) magnetic tape files;   (4 marks)
    (ii) magnetic disk files.   (10 marks)

(b) Give an illustration where each of the above media would be used for file storage, and provide a brief justification of your choice.   (6 marks)

32 BATCH AND REAL-TIME PROCESSING (20 marks)   12/89

Batch processing and real-time processing provide two extremely different methods of processing data to produce information.

Contrast these methods by describing one system using each approach. You should ensure that you comment on the hardware needed to support the systems, relative cost, and other advantages/ disadvantages of the two approaches.

33 DATA STORAGE ON DISK (20 marks)   6/91

Data can be stored on disk in various different ways, depending on the processing method to be used. This in turn will depend on the frequency of access, hit rate and size of the file.

Describe the different approaches to data storage on disk and in each case through use of an example explain why the method would be used.

34 BASIC REVISION QUESTION: TELECOMMUNICATIONS TERMS (12 marks)

Give a brief explanation, suitable for a manager, of the following telecommunications terms.

(a)	PABX	(4 marks)
(b)	PSS	(4 marks)
(c)	Baud rate	(4 marks)

35 DATA COMMUNICATION TERMS (20 marks)   6/90

Briefly explain the following terms which are used in data communications.

(a)	Accoustic coupler	(4 marks)
(b)	Multiplexor	(4 marks)
(c)	Modem	(4 marks)
(d)	Asynchronous	(4 marks)
(e)	Protocol	(4 marks)

36 NETWORKS (20 marks)   6/88

The modern *electronic office* is built around the installation of a *Local Area Network* which provides access to a *Wide Area Network*.

Required

(a) Explain what is meant by the *two* network terms.   (8 marks)

(b) Illustrate how these technical concepts support the various tasks performed in an electronic office.   (12 marks)

37 XAB LTD (20 marks)   12/87

XAB Ltd has twelve depots which supply 'Do it yourself' materials to the retail trade. Their systems are computerised using a distributed network of minicomputers.

(a) Define and explain briefly what is meant by the term *distributed data processing*.
                              (8 marks)
(b) List the features of a typical minicomputer used in a distributed network (8 marks)

(c) Name *four* systems which such a company may operate.   (4 marks)

38 MM ENTERPRISES (20 marks)   6/88

MM Enterprises, a finance house with 300 branches all over the world, carries out group data processing at its UK head office. Each week significant volumes of common information need to be distributed to each branch office. Telecommunication methods are too expensive and paper is too bulky.

(a) Identify and explain a suitable method for distributing this information. (10 marks)

(b) Describe the equipment required both at head office and branches to support your method. (10 marks)

39 IT TERMS (20 marks)

Write notes on the following terms which cover innovative applications of information technology.

(a) Electronic mail (10 marks)
(b) Facsimile transmission (10 marks)

40 SOFTWARE TERMINOLOGY (20 marks)   6/88

Explain the following terms as they apply to computer software.

(a) Source program (4 marks)
(b) Utility program (4 marks)
(c) Sub-routine (4 marks)
(d) Data base management system (DBMS) (4 marks)
(e) Data dictionary (4 marks)

41 BASIC REVISION QUESTION: PACKAGES (10 marks)

Define and explain the difference between the terms *application package* and *general purpose package* assuming that DBASE III+ and LOTUS 123 are examples of the latter.

42 OPERATING SYSTEMS (20 marks)   6/89

Operating systems are programs which enable the user to *drive* the computer. They are often quite technical so the latest versions use new techniques to make them *user friendly*.

(a) Briefly explain *five* tasks performed by an operating system. (10 marks)

(b) Define the term *user friendly*. (2 marks)

(c) The *mouse* is an innovation which makes systems easier to use. Describe how this works and explain *one* further technique which improves user friendliness. (8 marks)

43 WIMP OPERATING SYSTEM (20 marks)   12/90

Most modern microcomputers offer a user friendly operating system environment using a mouse, icons and pull-down menus.

(a) Briefly explain the role of the operating system in carrying out file maintenance activities on the computer. (8 marks)

(b) Describe how the mouse, icons and pull-down menus help the user to carry out these tasks in a simple way. (Use a screen diagram to illustrate your answer.) (12 marks)

44 BASIC REVISION QUESTION: SPREADSHEETS (10 marks)

Explain the features and functions of a typical spreadsheet program.

45 SPREADSHEET FACILITIES (20 marks)   6/90

The spreadsheet is an extremely useful software tool, often used by accountants.

Explain the typical facilities of a spreadsheet by working through an example. Your answer should include a sample model plus a description of the way in which this has been developed on the computer.

46 BASIC REVISION QUESTION: WORD PROCESSOR (10 marks)

Identify the factors which should be considered when selecting a suitable word processor.

47 WORD PROCESSING AND DESK-TOP PUBLISHING (20 marks)   12/89

Presentation is an increasingly important component of all business activity. *Word processing* is now readily accepted and used by many organisations for this purpose and *desk-top publishing* is now gaining in popularity.

(a) Describe the facilities offered by a typical word processing product.   (10 marks)

(b) Explain how desk-top publishing differs from word processing and briefly comment on its potential uses in an accounts office.   (10 marks)

48 DATA MANAGEMENT SOFTWARE (20 marks)   12/88

Data management software provides a powerful tool for use in today's office.

(a) Describe the features of such a package.   (10 marks)

(b) Explain *one* typical use of this software indicating the type of information that would be produced.   (6 marks)

(c) State *two* problems to be avoided when using this type of package.   (4 marks)

49 DATABASE MANAGEMENT (20 marks)   6/91

Database management software available on micro computers provides a powerful framework for development of data storage and retrieval systems. Maintenance of customer contact lists for mailing and other forms of communication is a typical application.

(a) Describe how you would use the features of a typical general purpose package of this type to build up a computer file of customer contacts.   (12 marks)

(b) Produce screen diagrams of two menu screens that you would expect the completed Customer Contact System to provide.   (8 marks)

50   SOFTWARE APPLICATIONS (20 marks)   6/91

Computer software can now be applied to a wide range of applications of value to an accounts department in any business.

Briefly explain and give a possible use of a software package in the following areas.

(a)   Desk top publishing (DTP)
(b)   Financial modelling
(c)   Expert systems
(d)   Presentation graphics.

51   BUSINESS SYSTEMS (20 marks)   12/90

You have recently joined a small manufacturing business and have discovered that you are the only member of staff who knows anything about computers.

(a)   Identify and briefly describe the objectives of *two* business systems excluding accounting/ payroll applications where computers might improve efficiency in this type of business.
(10 marks)

(b)   List *ten* questions you would ask of a supplier when seeking a software package to computerise one of these systems.
(10 marks)

52   INTEGRATED SYSTEMS: NOMINAL LEDGER   (20 marks)   6/88

Many software packages are advertised as fully *integrated* systems. A typical example would be an integrated sales, purchase and nominal ledger system.

(a)   Explain what is meant by the term *integrated* as it is used here.   (5 marks)

(b)   Describe the features you would expect to find in a *nominal ledger package* indicating how sales and purchase ledgers are linked into it.   (15 marks)

53   DECISION TABLE (20 marks)   6/86

You are investigating the stock system of ABC Ltd and you have decided to specify the reordering procedure in a decision table. The narrative description given by the clerk is as follows.

'I receive each requisition and consult my stock record to see whether sufficient stock is available to meet each item requested. If there is sufficient I adjust the balance on the stock record and write the quantity to be despatched on the requisition next to the quantity requested before passing it to the despatch clerk. I then check the adjusted balance to see if it has fallen below the reorder level.

If it has and there is no outstanding order on the factory I complete an order for that item. If there is insufficient stock to meet a requisition I write the quantity available on the form and pass it to despatch as normal but take a photocopy and put it in an outstanding requisitions file. I then adjust the balance on my stock record and generate an order if none is outstanding.

If an order is outstanding, I send an urge note to the factory to speed it up.

If there is no stock at all to meet a requisition I file it with outstanding requisitions. If nothing is on order, I generate one and telephone the factory to tell them it is coming. If there is an order I send an urge note as normal to chase it up.

Draw a decision table which fully describes this procedure.

54 FLOWCHART (20 marks)

A master file on magnetic tape holds a sequence of stock records in ascending order of the stock item key. Each item quotes current stock levels and minimum and maximum stock levels. Decks of cards are prepared from:

(i)   requisitions recording issues from stores; and
(ii) goods received notes.

Draw a program flowchart to show how you would process the updating of the stock file to give:

(a)   a list of all stock items, with the current stock level; and
(b)   a list of stock items to be re-ordered.

55 LOGICAL REPRESENTATION (20 marks)   6/89

A furniture retailer has the following credit policy.

For orders under £100 no credit is given.

For order between £100 and £750 inclusive, customers are offered terms over two years. New customers pay 15% interest but repeat customers pay only 12.5%.

For order over £750, previous customers pay the full rate of 15%, while new customers are referred to the credit control department for a decision.

Required

(a)   Draw a flow chart which presents this information in a logical form.   (12 marks)

(b)   Identify an alternative form for logical representation of these facts and present the decision in this form.   (8 marks)

56 BASIC REVISION QUESTION: LANGUAGES (15 marks)

(a)   What is a high level language?   (5 marks)

(b)   What do the following abbreviations (of high level languages) stand for, and why was each of the languages developed?

      (i)   FORTRAN
      (ii)   ALGOL
      (iii) PL/1
      (iv)   COBOL
      (v)   BASIC   (10 marks)

57 BASIC REVISION QUESTION: STRUCTURED TECHNIQUES (8 marks)

A particular requirement of your department is currently being programmed to run on the company computer. It is being written in a high level language using *structured techniques*.

What are structured techniques?

58 TERMINOLOGY IN PROGRAMMING (20 marks)   6/90

Computer users do not need to know much about programming but when they are dealing with system developers or sales organisations it is helpful if they know some of the terminology.

Briefly explain the meaning of the following terms.

(a) High level language   (5 marks)
(b) Object program   (5 marks)
(c) Logic error   (5 marks)
(d) Utility program   (5 marks)

59 DP DEPARTMENT (20 marks)   12/88

The diagram below represents an organisational structure of a DP department in a medium sized organisation running an *on-line* computer.

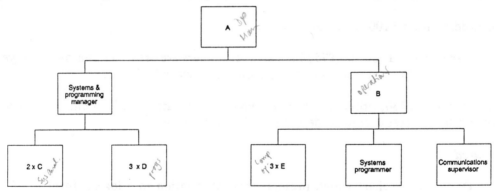

(a) State the job titles you would expect to find in boxes A to E.   (5 marks)

(b) Briefly describe the roles of post holders A, B, E.   (15 marks)

60 STAFF ROLES (20 marks)   12/89

In performing your role as accounting technician you may come into contact with the following specialist computing personnel. In each case briefly explain their role and provide an example of a situation where they would liaise with the accounts section.

(a) Systems analyst   (4 marks)
(b) File librarian   (4 marks)
(c) Data preparation supervisor   (4 marks)
(d) Computer maintenance engineer   (4 marks)
(e) Data control clerk   (4 marks)

61 DATA PROCESSING STAFF (20 marks)   6/91

In a large Data Processing department, there will be a number of staff who work in the operations section.

Describe the general role and two typical activities of *four* members of staff working in different parts of that section.

62 BASIC REVISION QUESTION: COMPUTER BUREAU (15 marks)

(a) What is a computer bureau?   (5 marks)

(b) State briefly some of the main advantages and disadvantages of the use of a computer bureau.   (10 marks)

63 COMPUTERISED PAYROLL (20 marks)   12/86

Your company has decided to computerise its weekly payroll and you have been asked to submit a brief report on alternative approaches. Produce an outline report covering advantages/disadvantages of using:

(a) a computer bureau;
(b) a dedicated micro in the wages office using a payroll package;
(c) a custom built system on the main computer.

64 PAYROLL AND BUREAU (20 marks)   6/90

Payroll is a data processing application which is often run by a computer bureau using a remote terminal installed on the client's premises.

(a) Briefly explain the features of a standard payroll system.   (8 marks)

(b) Describe the activities of a typical computer bureau.   (6 marks)

(c) Explain how this payroll application might work using a remote terminal. (6 marks)

65 INSTALLATION AND RUNNING COSTS (20 marks)   6/89

When a new computer system is acquired, the most obvious costs such as hardware and software are normally identified. Other costs are classified as either installation or running costs.

List and explain *five* extra costs under each of these headings.

66 ASSESSING A DP PROJECT (20 marks)   6/87

A member of the accounts department of a company which has a large central data processing department has had a bright idea for a new computerised system, which sounds good to his boss. The suggestion has been passed to the systems and programming manager for evaluation.

(a)   Explain the stages through which the idea will be passed before it is either rejected or accepted as a development project.   (10 marks)

(b)   Describe the role played by a systems and programming manager in a large DP department.
                                                                                          (10 marks)

67   BASIC REVISION QUESTION: RISKS AND CONTROLS

(a)   What are the risks to data?

(b)   What are:

   (i)   general controls?
   (ii)   application controls?

   Give one example of each.

68   CONTROLS OVER INPUT AND STORED DATA (14 marks)

(a)   Describe the controls which may be exercised over:

   (i)   computer input via a visual display unit (VDU); and
   (ii)   computer processing.   (7 marks)

(b)   Describe the objectives of the control function in relation to stored computer data and the methods available to achieve these objectives.   (7 marks)

69   BATCH CONTROL SYSTEM   (20 marks)   12/87

One of the biggest problems with batch processing of financial data on a computer system is control of data and errors to ensure that no data is lost, duplicated or updated to the wrong account.

List and briefly explain *ten* measures that should be included in a successful batch control system.   (20 marks)

70   DATA CONTROL   (20 marks)   6/91

Data control is of great importance in computer systems.

Explain the meaning of the following terms as they are used in a data processing context.

(a)   Check digit   (4 marks)
(b)   Validation report   (4 marks)
(c)   Reconciliation check   (4 marks)
(d)   File header   (4 marks)
(e)   Update error   (4 marks)

71 BASIC REVISION QUESTION: SECURITY (10 marks)

Explain what is meant by:

(a) grandfather, father, son technique;   (6 marks)
(b) 'passwords'   (4 marks)

72 PHYSICAL SECURITY (20 marks)   12/86

Physical security is of vital importance to computer users. As advisor to a small business, identify *five* different physical risks to which a computer system is exposed and describe the steps you would recommend to minimise these risks.

73 MINIMISE RISKS (20 marks)   12/89

When installing computers and computer systems particularly those dealing with personal and financial information, security of equipment and data is of vital importance. Identify *ten* different risks to which systems are exposed and briefly explain steps that can be taken to minimise these risks.

74 INTERNAL CONTROL IN A DP SYSTEM (20 marks)

Your company has its own mainframe computer and uses the on-line data entry method, through visual display units, for the processing of data. The purchasing department uses the system to process its orders to, and invoices from, suppliers. There are several steps involved in processing the data from the order/invoice to the final report taken from the computer to the purchasing department.

Use this background information to answer *four only* of the following.

(a) Purchase invoices from different suppliers are unlikely to be of the same design and format. How, therefore, can the data they contain be presented to your company's system?
                                                                            (5 marks)

(b) Explain what is meant by the term *verification* and how it may be carried out for the purchase orders.   (5 marks)

(c) Explain what is meant by the term *data validation* and how it may be carried out for purchase invoices.   (5 marks)

(d) Describe what information the final computer report could contain.   (5 marks)

(e) Outline some of the controls that will be necessary to run the purchase order/invoice system successfully.   (5 marks)

75 TEN CONTROLS (20 marks)   6/90

Results which are computer produced are expected to be reliable. Any information system must incorporate controls to ensure that this is the case.

List and briefly explain *ten* controls which may be implemented in a typical system.

76   SYSTEM SPECIFICATION (20 marks)   6/88

When a new computer based system is designed, one of the end products of the design process is a system specification.

Required

(a)   Explain the purpose of this document.   (4 marks)
(b)   List and briefly explain its contents.   (16 marks)

77   PROCEDURES MANUAL (20 marks)   6/89

When a new system is installed (eg a computerised Purchase Ledger) the user department running the system will require a procedures manual for training and reference purposes.

List and briefly explain the purposes of each section of such a manual using the above example if you wish.

78   DATA PROCESSING STANDARDS MANUAL   (20 marks)   12/90

When you are dealing with specialist computer staff, they often refer to the company Data Processing Standards manual.

(a)   Explain the purpose of such a manual.   (6 marks)

(b)   List the sections of a standards manual and briefly describe the contents of *four* of its sections.   (14 marks)

79   DP TERMS   (15 marks)

Required

(a)   Distinguish between the use of *Kimball tags* and *point of sale terminals* used in the retailing sector.   (5 marks)

(b)   Distinguish between *indexed sequential files* and *random access files* as used with magnetic disk filing systems.   (5 marks)

(c)   Distinguish between the terms *file dumping* and *file purging* and when would these techniques be used.   (5 marks)

80   EXPLAIN AND ILLUSTRATE (10 marks)

Write full explanatory notes, with examples and illustrations where appropriate, on the following.

(a)   Turnround documents.   (5 marks)
(b)   Exception reporting.   (5 marks)

81 SUNDRY TERMS   (20 marks)   12/89

Briefly explain the following data processing terms.

(a)	Minicomputer	(4 marks)
(b)	Viewdata	(4 marks)
(c)	Network	(4 marks)
(d)	Database	(4 marks)
(e)	Application package.	(4 marks)

SUGGESTED SOLUTIONS

SUGGESTED SOLUTIONS

1   BASIC REVISION QUESTION: COMPANY INFORMATION SYSTEMS

> *Tutorial note.* This question is very broad and lends itself to a number of interpretations. But probably the most sensible - and easiest - way to answer it is to consider the qualities of a good information system, and write about the corresponding weaknesses.

Five typical weaknesses in a company information system are:

(a) *noise* - ie information which is incomplete, irrelevant, unclear or excessive in quantity;

(b) *poor timing* - ie information is produced too late to be of any use (or perhaps even produced too frequently);

(c) *low value* - ie the cost of producing the information (the cost of operating the information system) may be greater than that of the information produced;

(d) *communication to the wrong person* - ie the system may produce perfectly good information, but fail in its purpose because it sends the information to somebody who does not want or need it;

(e) *loss of confidence* - ie once the system produces poor information, staff will not trust it in the future even if it then produces information. Distrust may even grow between staff if the poor information has been passed from one to another.

2   INFORMATION

(a) Errors may occur in the following ways.

   (i)   *Recording.* If a form is incorrectly filled in, the subsequent processing of the information will contain errors. Attention must be given to the proper design of forms and the training of the people who will be using them.

   (ii) *Data preparation.* Errors can occur as data is converted from a hard copy form to a computer readable form. Such errors may be transcripted errors, duplication, omissions etc. Controls to prevent those occurring would include pre-listing and batching, verification (two operators key in the same data which is then compared) etc.

   (iii) *Input.* The input device may misread the data. In a batch processing system the data vet program can perform range limit checks, existence and format checks, sequence and completeness checks, check digit verification etc.

   (iv) *Update stage.* Transactions data might be run against the wrong file or the wrong field within the right file. Again, in a batch processing system a master file update program will check that transaction record keys correspond with existing master file record keys, that any master file records that a transaction record is attempting to delete already exists, that a new (insertion) record has the same key field as an existing master file record, etc.

(b) 'Good' information must display the following characteristics.

   (i) *Purposeful.* The information should enable the user to do his job well and competently. Information which fulfills its purpose will be:

      1. *Relevant* (ie it should not contain irrelevant material that the user does not want, and only wastes time reading).

      2. *Complete* (ie it should not omit any information, thereby causing a wrong decision or judgement to be made).

      3. *Accurate* (ie it should not contain incorrect information, which could cause equally incorrect decisions to be made, and the level of accuracy should be appropriate to the decision).

      4. *Clear to the user* (ie it should not be phrased or set out in such a way that the user cannot understand it properly - and therefore cannot use it properly).

      5. *Trusted by the information user* (ie the user must have confidence in the information, otherwise he will not use it, and it might as well never have existed).

   (ii) *sent to the right person.* If the information is sent to someone who does not want it or who cannot use it, then it is just wasted.

   (iii) *sent by the right person.* If the sender and the user are far apart in the business, then the information may never arrive at its intended destination. Or if the sender and user simply do not get on, the information may never be used;

   (iv) *of the right amount.* There is no point in sending a vast amount of information to somebody if they are unable to make use of it all;

   (v) *timely.* Good information would not be communicated too late to be of any use, or at a time when the user does not want it;

   (vi) *current.* Good information is prepared from data that is up to date;

   (vii) *cost-effective.* Information should be provided at a cost which is less than the value of the benefits which it provides.

3 DATA PROCESSING SYSTEMS AND MIS

Tutorial note. Part (a) of this question is reasonably straightforward and you should be able to distinguish between an operational system and a management information system. A data processing system is a system used on a regular basis to process an organisation's routine transactions. An MIS provides information which has already been processed and has acquired value in the course of that processing. In part (b) you should review your examples to ensure that they *are* MIS decisions rather than operational decisions.

(a)   A data processing system is a system designed to take raw transaction data and to produce output of a routine or operational nature. For example, a sales order processing system, takes the basic details of the sales order, processes it, posts it to the sales ledger and sales account, and issues an invoice. Another example is payroll where operating data (eg time sheets) is fed into the system and operational output (payslips, BACS transfer tapes) are produced.

A management information system on the other hand is one designed to assist managers plan and control the business. It is an information system making use of all the available resources to provide managers at all levels in all functions with the information from all relevant sources to enable them to make timely and effective decisions for planning, directing and controlling the activities for which they are responsible.

A management information system is not really concerned with the detail of transaction data, but more with aggregates, ratios, trends, variances from budget and so forth. It is used to support decision making, and planning for the future of the business as well as the critical review of current operations. For example, an MIS would show which areas of the country were the most successful for selling goods.

(b)   The number of decisions which an MIS can influence is practically limitless.

(i)   *Commit sizeable funds to research and development*

For many large companies, R & D in the long term is necessary to develop new products and to ensure commercial advantage. Funding R & D would be authorised after its impact on the budget had been assessed, and whether any of the suggested products had a particular market. The MIS would detail estimated costs and benefits. The information would come from a variety of sources: from market research; from scientific research; from estimates of future interest rates and economic performance. The MIS would integrate these into one operation.

(ii)   *Buy a new computer system*

The MIS would indicate the costs of current operations which would be compared to the benefits that new investment would provide. Computer systems, it is felt, can reduce costs and also bring competitive advantage. Cost information would be provided by the MIS.

(iii)   *Close down part of the business*

The MIS would provide details of operating performance of part of the business, with particular trends and ratios made plain. The segment's performance over time would be shown, perhaps with comparative information from other business segments. Informal information would also be useful.

(iv)   *Appoint a credit controller*

An MIS could provide details of a worsening bad debt situation. Many companies lose money because their customers delay payment. This has a deleterious effect on cash flow. Bank overdraft and interest charges are much higher than they would be. An MIS can indicate the cost of a lax credit control policy. A credit controller's salary would be justified if the cash flow was improved sufficiently. An MIS would provide details of debtors ageing, bank charges, and estimated interest costs.

4   INFORMATION TERMS

> *Tutorial note.* The examiner noted that only one or two candidates understood the term 'query language' when this paper was set. It is a widely used tool in modern computing and there may well be future questions on *fourth-generation tools* if the paper is to keep pace with modern practice.

(a)   *Raw data*

Raw data is the term for the details of basic facts or events, which are input to a data processing system. Raw data has not been summarised, organised or processed by the system in any way. An example of raw data is an invoice generated as a result of a sale whose details are then entered to a sales ledger system. Another example is the results of a market research exercise: the questionnaires have to be aggregated and summarised before any useful information can be derived from them. Raw data is turned into information, something meaningful and useful to the recipient, by processing.

(b)   *Exception report*

One way of controlling a system is to examine those instances when it does not behave as it should, or where there are unexpected or unacceptable variances from plan. A more formal definition, offered by the CIMA, is that exception reporting is 'a system of reporting based on the exception principle which focuses attention on those items where performance differs significantly from standard or budget'. Small variations are to be expected, as a plan can rarely be more than an approximation.

An example of an exception report is a list of costs that have exceeded budget by a defined percentage, and thus need management attention.

(c)   *Strategic information*

Strategic information is used by senior managers to plan the objectives of their organisation and to see whether those objectives are being met in practice.

Strategic information can be generated within the organisation. Such information relating to a commercial organisation can include the overall profitability of the organisation as a whole, or different parts of it. For example, a company producing a large number of goods might wish to know which are the most profitable, or which markets are the most valuable.

Other strategic information can be obtained from outside the organisation (eg long term social trends, state of the economy etc).

(d)   *Graphical information*

Graphical information is information presented in pictorial or diagrammatic form. Pictures, charts, graphs or diagrams are often easier to grasp than a row of numbers although the message (eg relative profits of different segments of a business) is the same. Graphical techniques are used to present relatively abstract information in a way that is easy to understand. It is possible to print graphs from numerical data. Moreover, many computer programs can display data in graphical form on screen.

Graphics can be presented by some spreadsheet packages. It is especially useful in the writing of management reports, or in the presentation of complex financial information to those who may not be able to understand it easily.

(e) *Query language*

A query language is a type of software used to interrogate a store of information for items that conform to the user's specified criteria. Query languages are most commonly used with databases. In a database, the structure of data items does not depend on any particular use or application, so the instruction in the query language is used by the database management system to extract the information required. For example, in a database containing employee details, a query language could be used to extract information relating to employees over 55 years old.

5 BASIC REVISION QUESTION: FILE TYPE

(a) Sequential
(b) Low
(c) Disk
(d) Indexed sequential
(e) Disk

6 BASIC REVISION QUESTION: PAYROLL MASTER FILE

The amount of information held on the payroll master file will depend on whether some employee information is held on another file or on the payroll file - eg is a person's home address, annual holiday entitlement and sickness history recorded on a personnel file or added to the payroll file record? And is the gross pay (and overtime rate etc) for a grade of worker included on a separate pay scales file, or is an individual's gross pay rate kept on the payroll file record itself? etc. The solution below is merely intended to give you an idea of what might be included on the payroll file. It is not a unique 'correct' solution.

Payroll file. The records relate to individual employees. The files in each record might be:

> Employee number - key field
> Name
> National Insurance number
> Department code
> Gross annual pay (salaried employees)
> Hourly rate (wage earners)
> Income tax code
> Pension deductions
> Union membership contributions
> Other deductions (voluntary subscriptions)
> Pay details for the year to date:
> > Gross pay to date;
> > Income tax to date;
> > National Insurance to date;
> > Other deductions to date;
> > Cumulative entitlements for the year to date;
> > Holiday pay;
> > Commission/bonus.

7 FIXED ASSETS ACCOUNTING SYSTEM

(a) *Data fields in an assets master file*

(i) The key field will probably be an *asset number*, although in a database system there would be a variety of ways to access the information.

(ii) Asset *category*, eg motor vehicles, office equipment, sometimes to considerable detail. The law requires certain types of asset to be disclosed separately in a company's annual report and accounts.

(iii) Physical *location* of the asset. This may simply be the office site where the asset is situated or, in large organisations the country where the asset resides.

(iv) Original *cost* of the asset. The company has to ensure that the cost of the asset is correctly recorded. If the asset was purchased in a foreign currency, the correct exchange rate would be given.

(v) Any *revaluations* of cost. Freehold property is likely to be revalued to reflect its current worth.

(vi) *Depreciation provided* to date.

(vii) *Date* of acquisition of the asset.

(viii) Estimated useful *life* of the asset. An asset will wear out in a given period of time.

(ix) *Method of depreciation.* A company may charge different amounts of depreciation in a given year.

(x) *Cost centre* to which depreciation should be charged. The depreciation on a salesperson's car will be charged to the sales department.

(b) (i) When as asset is acquired, the file is updated by the input of an appropriate master record with most of the fields in (a) above.

(ii) Asset transfer between departments requires both the details of physical location and the cost centre to be changed.

(iii) Revaluation of an asset may require a restatement of cost, or it may arise out of a revised estimate of the asset's useful life. The records will have to be updated accordingly.

(iv) Sale of an asset requires its deletion from the entire fixed assets accounting system, and some means of calculating the profit or loss on disposal.

You could also use as examples:

(v) Periodic depreciation charge. Depreciation may be charged monthly. This may affect the net book value of the asset.

(vi) Write off of assets. The procedure is similar to that of a sale, in that the asset will be deleted from the system.

(c) (i) *Assets listed by cost centre*

(*Key* MV: Motor Vehicles; OE: Office Equipment)

Cost centre	Asset no.	Category	Net book value £
Sales dept	101 102 298	MV MV OE	
Accounts dept	103 299	OE OE	

(ii) *Assets: monthly depreciation charge*

Asset no.	Cost centre	Cost b/f £	Dep'n b/f £	Current period dep'n £	Dep'n c/f £	Net book value b/f £	Net book value c/f £
101 102 103 · · 298 299 · ·	Sales Sales Accounts Sales Accounts						

8 STOCK CONTROL SYSTEM

(a) *Fields on stock master file*

    (i) Stock reference number, for identification.

    (ii) Stock description, for printing physical stock counts.

    (iii) Unit of stock (eg dozens, hundreds), for reference.

    (iv) Current balance, for monitoring.

    (v) Cost price, for valuation.

    (vi) Selling price, for invoicing, and for valuation if less than (v).

(vii) Standard cost, for budgeting and valuation.

(viii) Dates of usage, for control purposes.

(ix)   Economic reorder quantity - amount to be ordered at (x).

(x)   Re-order level, to generate automatic orders.

(xi)   Quantity on order, for planning.

(xii) Delivery lead time, to allow production and/or sales planning.

(xiii) Supplier reference number, for ease of accounting, creditors files etc.

(xiv) Warehouse details

(b) *Regular transactions to update a stock master file*

   (i)   Stock *requisition* occurs when an item of stock is allocated to a sale (if finished goods), or to a stage in the production process.

   (ii)   *Additions* to stock occur when supplies are received.

   (iii) *Transfers* to and from different stock categories may occur when an item of stock is transferred from raw materials into work in progress, or from work in progress to finished goods.

   (iv)   The stock master file may permit certain *automatic adjustments* to be made. If wastage occurs normally, this may be accounted for within the stock master files as an adjustment for estimated wastage.

   (v)   Adjustments to stock records may be made after a *physical stock count*. These adjustments may affect quantity if the actual stock levels differ from recorded stock levels.

   (vi)   Alternatively, the adjustment may be made to the *value* of stock, if it is obsolete or in poor condition.

   (vii) Changes to the 'cost' of an item in stock may be made if the supplier increases prices. If the company maintains a 'standard costing system' where stock is valued at a set amount for a specified period, then changes may be made at the end of that period.

   (viii) *New stock lines* may come into production requiring updating the file for the new category of stock.

(c) *Reports that the system might produce*

   (i)   A paper based report, giving the amounts and values of every product line at a particular time.

(ii) A paper based report detailing movements in product lines over a period, giving with references, goods received notes and despatch notes.

(iii) A screen based report might allow enquiry into the situation regarding a particular item of stock without the time taken to print out a detailed report. A screen report, depending, of course, on whether the system is on-line or batch processed, would be an up-to-date indicator of the stock movements on a particular line at any time.

9 SALES ORDER PROCESSING SYSTEM

> *Tutorial note.* This question follows a model which has been used by the examiner on several occasions. You should have noticed that part (a) requires answers to two distinct questions. A satisfactory answer to part (c) must acknowledge the presence of the telephone rather than making general comments about credit control.

(a) To process a sales order, enough information must be given to the sales clerk to ensure that the right quantities of the right product at the agreed price are despatched to the customer. The information required over the phone would include:

- customer name;
- customer account number, if any;
- customer address, if a new customer;
- description of stock item required;
- stock part number, if customer has a list;
- quantity of stock required;
- when the stock is required (if flexibility is available).

The sales order entry clerk would enter the relevant information so that details of the account can be displayed on screen. The clerk might check on the stock master file whether the items are available. Details of the order may be written down for authorisation first before they are input. Once input, details of the order details would be used to update the stock master file, and once the goods were delivered, if the company does not insist on payment in advance, the customer file would also be updated with the invoiced amount.

(b) The likely fields on a customer file are:

- account number;
- name;
- address;
- delivery address;
- credit limit;
- current balance outstanding;
- transactions for current period, and outstanding amounts from previous periods, and cash receipts not allocated to invoices;
- any special terms.

(c) The system could be used to reduce the risks of bad debts in the following ways.

- Any particular problem with a customer's account can be flagged on screen when the sales clerk is making enquiries.

- Credit limits are input to the computer which notifies the user if an order means a credit limit is exceeded. This is done before an order is accepted.

- If transactions details are held on file, an *aged debtors analysis* can be produced (giving the dates of invoices outstanding and when they are paid) so that customers with possible payment problems can be identified early, and credit restricted.

(Note: only *two* suggestions were required)

10 SALES LEDGER SYSTEM

(a) The inputs of a computerised sales ledger system can generally be grouped into two types: amendments and transaction data. Some typical inputs are listed below:

    (i) *Amendments:*

        1   to customer details: change of address, credit limit etc;
        2   insertion of new customers;
        3   deletion of 'non-active' customers.

    (ii) *Transaction data* referring to:

        1   sales transactions for invoicing;
        2   customer payments;
        3   credit notes;
        4   adjustments (debit or credit items).

(b) The sales ledger files consists of individual records for each customer account. Some data held on the record is standing data and is changed infrequently, while other data is variable data and will change as the sales ledger is updated.

    (i) *Standing data* includes the customer's name, address, account number and credit limit. Also included in standing data is the account sales analysis code and the account type (ie open item or balance forward).

    (ii) *Variable data* includes transaction data, a description of the transaction (eg sale, credit note, etc), the transaction code (eg to identify payment period allowed), debits, credits and balance.

(c) Other processes carried out by a sales ledger system include:

    (i) updating (where new details are added to the file);

    (ii) calculating (where balances are worked out and amended);

    (iii) analysing (where sales are analysed according to the sales analysis codes);

    (iv) sorting (where records or transactions are sorted into a required sequence);

    (v) producing output (eg customer lists, statements, sales analysis reports etc).

(d) Outputs from a computerised sales ledger system are numerous, some produced daily and others more frequently. Typical outputs are:

(i) day book listing - which is a list of all transactions posted each day;
(ii) statements - probably produced monthly for customers;
(iii) invoices;
(iv) customer lists - eg customer address lists on labels for despatching price lists;
(v) sales analysis reports;
(vi) aged debtors list;
(vii) debtors reminder letters.

11 SALES LEDGER ENQUIRY SCREEN

> *Tutorial note.* There were two ways you could have approached this question. Doing part (b) first would have given you all the fields you needed to draw up your sample screen. Alternatively, you might have found it easier to draw the screen first, as you could have based it on one with which you are familiar at work. This would have made it easier to answer part (b) as you could have just read all the fields you needed off the screen.

A sales ledger enquiry can be used to provide information about customer accounts. Depending on the sophistication of the system, this can include a list of balances, or a breakdown, by unpaid invoices, of the balance on a customer's account. The invoices are likely to be listed in chronological order so that if necessary an age analysis can be prepared from the summary data.

(a) A typical sales ledger enquiry screen is outlined below.

```
CQQ HOLDINGS PLC DEBTORS LEDGER
INSTRUCTION: ACCOUNT ENQUIRY
DATE:        01 JULY 19X0

U-WANT BOOKS                    ACCOUNT  353QU
DISCOUNT HOUSE
PLAGIARY STREET                 PAYMENT TERMS        60 DAYS
PULPHAM                         CREDIT               £20,000
BUCKS                           CREDIT AVAILABLE     £7,765
                                ACCOUNT FROZEN? (Y/N)    N

DATE      TRANSACTION  REFERENCE  STATUS    DR     CR     BALANCE
          INVOICE      0483                 8,200         8,200
30/4/X0   INVOICE      2043                 7,000         15,200
          C/NOTE       081        ALLOC            1,200  14,000
13/5/X0   INVOICE                            2,365        16,365
27/5/X0   PAYMENT      34487      ALLOC            7,000  9,365
28/5/X0   INVOICE      6348                 1,000         10,365
15/6/X0   INVOICE      6451                   940         11,295
20/6/X0   INVOICE      7850                   930         12,235

       Over 90 days   61-90 days   31-60 days   0-30 days   TOTAL
                      7,000.00      3,365.00     1,870.00    12,235.00

       ENQUIRY MENU F1    MAIN MENU F2
```

(b) *Data fields*

As the screen displays most of the detailed account transactions on the sales ledger, then it must contain many of the fields of the sales ledger file. These fields are listed below.

For each account

Account number.
Customer name.
Customer address.
Payment terms (days).
Credit limit.
Credit available.
Account frozen (Yes or No). No further transactions would be permitted if there were persistent late payment of bills, or over stepping of credit limit.

For each transaction

Date.
Reference number.
Type (eg invoice or credit note or payment received).
Amount.
Status (payments might be allocated to particular invoices).

Note that the debtors ageing information is not a field of data in its own right, as it is simply a programmed calculation from data already available.

(c) *Transactions*

The following transactions are used to keep the file up to date. Items (i) to (iii) are transactions data. Items (iv) to (vi) are amendments to standing data. (*Tutorial note.* You were only required to identify two transactions.)

(i) Invoices detail sales to the customer, and amounts outstanding.

(ii) Payments received clear the debt.

(iii) Credit notes correct errors, or notify the customer of a reduction in the debt (eg because of goods returned) have to be recorded in the ledger.

(iv) Amendments to the credit limit indicate what credit a customer is given. This might be increased or reduced.

(v) The payment terms might change.

(vi) The customer might change address.

(d) *Decisions*

(*Tutorial note.* A number of decisions are made as a result of this information. You were required to specify *two*.)

(i) Increase or reduce credit limit as a result of a customer's reliability and payment record.

(ii) Stop selling, on a temporary or permanent basis, to a customer with a poor payment record.

(iii) Send reminder letters to slow payers, or take more drastic action (eg solicitor's letters, legal action, debt collection agency, bailiffs).

(iv) Change payment terms.

12 FILE PROCESSING TERMS AND DIAGRAM

> *Tutorial note.* This is a fairly straightforward question. Remember when preparing flowcharts to make use of a stencil or template. The rubric on the examination paper specifically refers to this and the examiner will not be impressed by freehand sketches and indeterminate shapes.

(a) A *file* is a collection of data records with similar characteristics, for example a file of purchase ledger transactions or of customer details. There are a variety of types of file for example:

- transaction files which store transactions to be processed;
- master files, which contains standing data, and cumulative brought forward data are updated by transaction files;

Database files contain data which can be used by several different applications.

A file is made up of records with similar characteristics. A *record* is a collection of fields relating to one logically definable unit of business information. Examples of records are:

- a sales ledger transaction (eg payment received);
- standing data related to a customer (eg name, address, account code).

A record is made up of fields. A *field* is a combination of characters representing one item of data. For example:

- the standing data record related to a customer mentioned above contains a number of fields (the customer's name is a field);
- the value of a purchase invoice is a field.

We have seen that a file is a collection of data records with similar characteristics, and have give some examples. However, how do we identify each record uniquely and efficiently? In a sales ledger, you could simply identify a record by customer name; but if the name is common to two customers, there might be confusion between them. Alternatively, invoices might be identified solely by value, but then there will be confusion between invoices of the same value. Every record needs a unique identifier: each customer on the sales ledger will have an account code; each transaction will have a unique transaction reference.

This code or transaction reference is used to identify the record on file. The code is one of the fields in the record, and as it used for this purpose it is known as the *key field*.

Records often need to be sorted before they are processed or used to update a master file. For example a file of sales transaction will be sorted into customer account number order before the customer master file is updated. Sorting is particularly necessary for batch processing applications, especially where magnetic tape is the storage medium.

(b) Flowchart

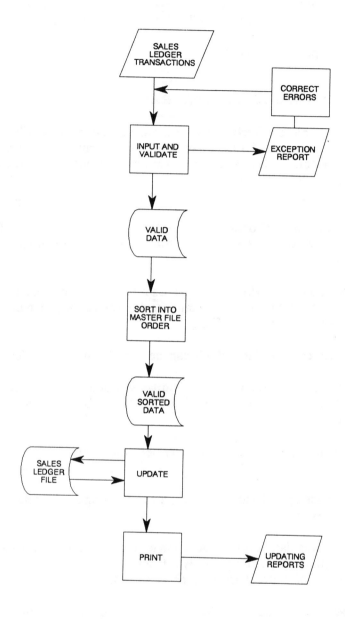

This flowchart assumes that the sales ledger master file is on disk, so it updated by overlay. Sorting transactions data is still useful, as it speeds up the updating process later.

In this flowchart, the sales ledger transaction records are sorted into the order of the key fields by which records on the master file are organised.

13 PROCESSING TERMS

(a) *Batch processing*

This is said to occur when a group of similar routine transactions is processed in one processing operation.

There are three stages in processing:

(i)   data collection;
(ii)   input;
(iii) processing.

The important distinguishing feature in batch processing is that (i) and (ii) are separate operations from (iii). Operations (i) and (ii) can, however, be combined.

For example, invoices raised in a small branch of a large chain of shops might be written out by hand. The invoices are then grouped together. This is stage (i). The shopkeeper's assistant then takes the invoices and converts this data into machine-sensible form, eg by typing the relevant details on to a magnetic tape. This is stage (ii). The collection of invoices and their inputting has been in batches. The tape is then couriered to the company's head office, and run into the computer as a separate operation. In many supermarkets, the transaction is recorded when a laser reads the bar codes on items sold. This is an example of on-line data capture, combining stages (i) and (ii).

However, the input transactions may be entered *directly* into the main computer system over a period of time, but processing may not begin until they have been batched together. This is referred to as on-line batch processing. Data is stored before processing in a file separate from the master file which it will update.

(b) *On-line processing*

Two types of on-line processing can be identified.

(i)   *On-line batch processing* occurs when data is input directly into the main computer system. However, the data is stored in a file separate from the master file which it will update.

(ii)   *On-line real-time* processing is said to occur when the data is processed as soon as it is captured and input to the main computer system. On-line real-time processing requires magnetic disk based hardware. Data might be entered on remote terminals connected to the main computer system by cable or the telecommunications network. The hardware is likely to be more expensive than in a batch processing system.

With on-line real-time processing, data is up-to-date, but there is greater scope for error, in that input data updates the master files immediately. An example is a theatre booking system, where the records are updated immediately a booking is made.

(c) *Distributed data processing*

This occurs when data is processed on a distributed system. A system is said to be distributed when a number of separate, *autonomous* computer processors and peripheral equipment are linked together over a communications network.

(*Tutorial note:* we are *not* referring to a system where data is input at several terminals and sent down to one main computer. There are *several* computers in a distributed system.)

Data can be processed on some or all of the computers, either independently or interactively. Interactive data processing means that the same data processing task is done by more than one computer.

Files can either be held centrally or locally, on the individual computers in the departments that use them. Files on one computer can be interrogated by other computers in the system, subject to confidentiality controls, when necessary.

Distributed systems offer local autonomy and flexibility, with the benefits of a unified system. An example is when a computer in the sales ledger department processes sales information data and sends the results to the accounts department. To summarise, this form of processing provides an information system that is decentralised but not fragmented into totally separate parts. Processing is distributed between different processors; files can be held in different locations (although some may be held centrally); management control over data processing is therefore decentralised.

Distributed systems are likely to become more common as powerful computer hardware becomes cheaper. In particular, the wide availability of minicomputers and inexpensive microcomputers has made distributed processing more cost effective.

(d) *Timesharing*

This occurs where one computer appears to perform several different jobs concurrently, on instructions from different users.

Timesharing is possible because the time taken by the CPU (central processing unit) to process instructions is much less than the time taken for data to be transferred between the CPU and the computer's peripheral devices (eg a VDU). When a user keys in instructions at the keyboard, these are relayed to the CPU, executed, and the results are sent as 'output' to the VDU screen. The CPU is not working when it is waiting for instructions, and when it has sent the output to the VDU.

Timesharing works by allocating this spare time to another user, whose programs may require the processing of completely different files. The CPU switches between different programs and files. In times of heavy use, the instructions may have to be stored in a queue before processing. A large timesharing system might have hundreds of terminals.

Timesharing is organised by software resident in the computer's main memory. This software is called the *timesharing supervisor*. The flow between the CPU and peripheral devices is controlled by other software, known as the *transfer monitor*.

14 PURCHASE LEDGER SYSTEM

> *Tutorial note.* Another input-process-output question. In a question like this you must check carefully whether the examiner has asked for details of, for example, input *devices* or input *transactions*.

(a) Input transactions in a typical purchase ledger system include:

- setting up account;
- deleting account;
- routine file maintenance (eg supplier address);
- recording of purchase invoices;
- recording of payment;
- account adjustments;
- contras with sales ledger;
- recording of credit notes received;
- audit adjustments.

(*Tutorial note*: only *three* input transactions were required.)

(b) Data fields on a master file include:

- supplier code number;
- supplier name;
- supplier address;
- terms normally offered by supplier (eg discounts for early payment;
- credit limit offered by supplier;
- current balance owing;
- unmatched transactions (eg invoices for which no goods received notes have been raised, for whatever reason);
- transactions over a specified period (current month, if the file is updated monthly);
- for unmatched transactions from previous periods and for current period, each invoice record to include details of amounts, VAT etc.

(*Tutorial note*: only *eight* fields were required.)

(c) Processes other than storage and retrieval include:

- sort (if batch processing);
- dumping (copies on to another file for safe keeping);
- purging;
- validation of input data;
- control totalling;
- updating of master file by alteration of outstanding balances for example, to take account of inputs;
- selection of items for output, under program control.

A wide variety of processing can be achieved, depending on the programs written.

(*Tutorial note*: only *four* processes were required.)

(d) Typical outputs are as follows.

- Exception/rejection reports after data validation.

  These detail items that were in excess of certain limits or were in some way unusual (exception reports), or items that were not processed at all for some reason (rejection reports).

- Screen output as a result of file enquiry.

  Users might wish to know the status of a particular account at a particular time.

- Printed output of master file.

  The master file and all details thereon could be printed regularly. This might be useful for audit trail, or investigation of some items.

- Printed open items report.

  Unmatched transactions might be printed out for further investigation.

- Statements.

  An regular periods, an organisation may send its suppliers statements of balances on its accounts, in case of disagreement.

(*Tutorial note*: only *two* outputs were required.)

15 BATCH PROCESSING FLOWCHART

Stages included in producing a transaction file using a batch processing method

(a) Originating documents are raised clerically by source location/office, eg invoices, payment instructions, stores issue notes.

(b) Documents are then passed to section head for clerical checking, validation procedures and authorisation.

(c) Documents gathered together and checked for authorisation. Then, like documents are put into batches containing approximately equal numbers of vouchers.

(d) For each batch a batch control slip is prepared by the originating location showing batch number document count, batch totals (eg invoice totals) and appropriate hash totals (eg total of invoice numbers). The main purposes of the batch control slip are:

  (i) to ensure that all batches of documents are processed (using the batch serial number); and

  (ii) to ensure that all documents within each batch are processed (using the document total, batch total and hash total).

(e) Batch numbers are issued serially from the batch control book where all details from the batch control slip are also recorded.

(f) Batches are then sent to data preparation where details from the batch control slip are recorded in a record control book. Any batches missing from a series are reported and investigated.

(g) Document and control details are keyed onto magnetic tape. This information is keyed in a second time for verification and elimination of transcription errors.

(h) The data tape is passed to the operations room for input to the computer. The first run carries out validation and edit checks and produces a listing of all valid documents with a document count and total value. A similar reject count is also produced. All batch totals are reconciled to the original input totals.

(i) Batches containing rejected documents are identified and the rejected documents removed. Totals are recalculated and entered in the batch control book.

(j) Rejected documents are themselves batched and returned to the originating location where batch control totals are amended. Rejected documents are investigated and amended for re-input as soon as possible.

(k) Data is sorted into master-file order.

Once validated, all valid documents are run for a second time in concert with appropriate master files to produce the transaction file.

(l) Various control reports may be produced which are reconciled with the batch control records held in data preparation and by the originating location. Any discrepancies will be investigated.

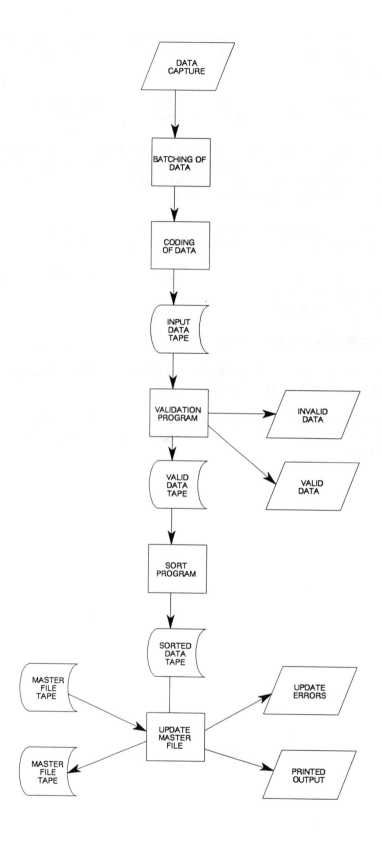

16   BASIC REVISION QUESTION: BATCH AND INTERACTIVE PROCESSING

(a)   A batch processing system is one in which transaction data, usually in large bulk and divided into batches (for administrative convenience) is processed periodically. All the transaction data goes through the processing stages together, and the results of one item cannot be found until the results of all the items are known.

An interactive processing system is one in which data is handled on a transaction-processing basis - ie where each transaction can be entered and processed individually and so records on file are kept up to date. The 'interactive' nature of this processing is that not only is transaction data fed into the system, but also data can be communicated by the system to the user at the same time. This means that there can be a two-way transmission of data during the input process and the user and computer communicate with each other in 'conversational mode'. Files are updated as transactions occur, and enquiries can be dealt with by providing an immediate response. The term 'real-time' processing can be used to describe this feature of processing.

(b)   (i)   *Entry of data:* with batch processing, transaction data is built up over a period of time, during which it is converted into a machine-sensible form within batches. Entries within each batch are identified by a batch code number and 'batch header' data is also input containing control information relating to each batch. Often, transactions of the same type are grouped within a batch. Data is then entered for processing in bulk.

With interactive processing, there is random input of data at random time intervals, often from one of several remote terminals.

(ii)   *Validation of input:* with batch processing, data validation is carried out on input data, often within a separate 'data vet' program, and a large number of checks are carried out on various items within each control record. As much validation as possible is done by computer so as to avoid the likelihood of large numbers of errors with a 'manual' validation on bulk volumes of data.

With interactive processing, some data validation can be carried out by program, possibly within the computer or within the terminal itself. However, programmed validation checks tend to be fairly limited in scope and a greater onus is placed on the visual checks on input by the terminal user.

(iii)   *Correction of errors:* with batch processing, errors are reported for all the batched input at the same time. In urgent cases, errors can be corrected by computer operating/administration staff in consultation with the user or customer. In non-urgent cases, error reports will be sent back to the user for investigation, in which case the correction of errors will be deferred until the next batches of data are processed.

With interactive processing, any data validation or other errors that are identified when the data is input and processed will be reported (normally on a VDU screen) to the user for immediate corrective action. Errors can therefore be corrected by the user 'on the spot'.

(iv)   *Order of transactions:* with batch processing, transaction data can be sorted into an order that facilitates processing and checking. Sorting can be manual and/or carried out within a sort program. Manual sorting would involve the organisation of data into batches of like items. A sort program would be used to pre-sort transaction data into the same order as master file data, prior to master file updating. The purpose of pre-sorting would be to reduce total processing time, and would probably not be required where the ratio of transaction records to master file records is low.

With interactive processing, the input of transaction data is random and there is no structured order of transactions.

(v) *Back-up facilities for master file:* with batch processing, back-up facilities for master files are provided by:

(1) duplicate copies of the master file being made, but also

(2) the grandfather-father-son system of file security. If the current master file has been corrupted, a new file can be re-created by re-running the previous one (or two) batch process computer runs.

With interactive processing, back-up facilities for the master file can only be provided by taking occasional copies of the file. If a file subsequently becomes corrupted, all the transactions input since the last copy was made would be lost.

(vi) *Back-up facilities for transactions:* with batch processing, back-up facilities for transactions, in the event of corruption of the transactions file, can be provided by:

(1) taking copies of original transactions input files and/or keeping the original input (eg retaining punched cards which could be re-used for processing if necessary);

(2) producing printed records of transactions input, in batch order, as 'check records'.

With interactive processing, there are usually no back-up facilities for transactions because transactions are processed on to the master file instantaneously and so the need for back-up is restricted to master files. However, if required, a printout of transactions can be produced.

17 BASIC REVISION QUESTION: COMPUTER MODEL

(a) *The in-tray:* this will be any device by which data is captured and input to the system. In a computer system the device could be punched cards, punched paper tape, magnetic tape or a disk, or a document reader, a keyboard with VDU, an electronic point of sale device, a card or badge transmission device, etc.

(b) *The out-tray:* after data has been processed it must be output to the user of the information. In a computer system output devices might be line printers, optical or laser printers, desk-top printers, microfilm or microfiche, or VDUs.

(c) *The filing cabinet:* this represents the external storage device where standing data and program instructions are retained, to be accessed when required. Magnetic tapes and disks are the most frequently used media for external storage, the choice depending on whether or not direct access will be required (disk), whether the 'hit rate' is high, etc.

(d) *The table:* this represents the computer's memory. The various items on the table are analogous to the computer memory holding the current program instructions and the items of data currently being processed according to the program. When the computer is switched off – ie the table is cleared – those items are erased from the memory.

(e) *The procedures manual:* this in analogous to the program currently lodged in the computer's memory. The program instructs the computer as to how to process the data currently input. If this instruction program were not there, data could still be input but the computer would not be able to process is so as to produce the output required.

18 BASIC REVISION QUESTION: CENTRAL PROCESSING UNIT

(a)

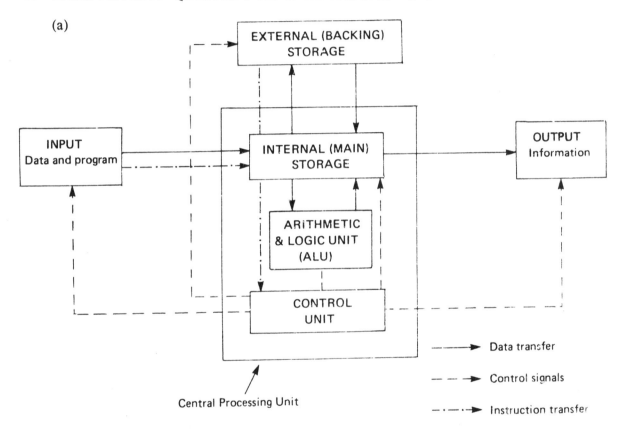

As indicated by the above diagram, the major components of a computer system are:

(i) *Input units*
Before a computer can process information the data must be introduced into the machine in a form which it can understand (direct reading of special figures on documents, magnetic tape, floppy disk, VDU and keyboard etc).

(ii) *Control unit*
This is the portion of the central processor hardware which directs the sequence of operations, interprets the coded instructions which are obtained from memory and initiates the proper commands to the computer circuits to execute instructions. This supervises all the processes and controls the activities of the configuration (eg input units to internal storage; internal storage to output units; external storage to CPU; the CPU to external storage; and one part of storage to another).

(iii) *Memory unit (internal storage)*
A computer is able to store information, usually in integrated circuits on silicon chips, and it can produce this stored information when requested to do so by the program.

(iv) *Arithmetic/logic unit*
The prime advantage to be gained from the use of a computer is the speed with which it can make calculations and comparisons. This is done in the arithmetic/logic unit.

(v) *External storage (backing storage)*
As the internal storage is usually insufficiently large to hold all data, files and programs additional storage is necessary. The information is stored on magnetic tapes, disks etc and called on when required.

(vi) *Output units*
The computer produces information from its output unit in the form of punched cards, punched paper tape, magnetic tape, VDUs etc. This information must be translated and printed. On-line or off-line printers may be used according to the volume and speed of output required.

(b) Whereas the normal, everyday decimal method of counting is based on the number 10, binary counting is based on the number two. This has two immediate effects on how numbers are represented in binary:

(i) the only symbols used are 0 and 1 (2 cannot be used because that is the base number, in much the same way as there is no single symbol representing ten in the decimal system);

(ii) instead of the columns of a number representing units, tens, hundreds, thousands and so on, the columns represent units, twos, fours, eights, etc. So 10101101, for instance in the number 173 written out in binary:

Binary	1	0	1	0	1	1	0	1	
Decimal	128	-	32	-	8	4	-	1=	173

(c) A computer's operations depend on simple two state devices (eg a transistor, like a switch, which may be either on or off) and so it cannot process data given in alphabetic characters or decimal number. However, the two states can be conveniently expressed by the number 0 and 1, 0 for 'off' and 1 for 'on'. Any piece of data or instruction must be coded in these symbols before processing can commence. Binary counting, consisting as it does of 0's and 1's only, is therefore ideally suited for computer operations.

(d) (i) ROM stands for *read only memory*.

Read only memories are memory chips into which data is written at the time of their manufacture. New data cannot be written into the memories, and so the data they contain are unchangeable and irremovable, even if the microprocessor's power is cut off. ROM is therefore described as 'non-volatile' or 'permanent memory'. ROMs can only be used when it is known that the data they contain need never be altered. The start-up program, known as a 'bootstrap' program, is always held in a form of a ROM. Similarly, the interpreter program is frequently held on ROM.

(ii) RAM stands for *random access memory*.

Random access memories are memory chips found in microprocessors. Data can be written or read from random access memory and RAMs correspond to the main memory of a conventional computer. RAM can be defined as 'memory with the ability to access any location in the memory in any order with the same speed'. Random access is an essential requirement for the main memory of a computer. Small home computers may be advertised, for example, as, say, 64K RAM, 32K ROM, which refers to the size of main storage and the type of memory it consists of. Unlike ROM, RAM is volatile which means that anything held in the memory is lost when the computer is switched off.

19 HARDWARE TERMINOLOGY

Tutorial note. This question offers a good base for marks with terms such as RAM, hard disk, floppy disk and processor. You might have found slightly less inspiration when tackling 'resolution' and 'ports'. A port is simply a socket on the computer allowing peripheral devices to be connected to it.

Intel 8088 16-bit processor

Intel is a major US manufacturer of silicon chips and processors. The microprocessor is the part of a computer that carries out operations on data, executing instructions, and controlling the flow of information. The microprocessor is contained on an integrated circuit, and is made out of silicon. Data in a computer is held in the form of electronic signals, represented by bits (binary digits). A computer can only process so many bits at a time. A 16-bit processor can process 16 bits at a time.

256K bytes RAM

A byte is 8 bits, and a kilobyte is 1024 bytes. RAM stands for Random Access Memory. Random Access Memory is memory that can be both read and written to. The fact that it can be written to means that it can be altered. Memory stores data in electronic form, in bits. As a byte is commonly used as a basic unit of data (eg a character), memory size is given in the number of bytes that memory can store. A 256K byte RAM memory can store 256 x 1,024 = 262,144 bytes of information. The RAM memory is normally volatile, which means that its contents are erased when the computer is switched off. In the context of the question RAM memory refers to the immediate access store in the CPU.

20 Mb hard disk storage

A hard disk is a storage device used in many microcomputers. It is stored in a container that is hermetically sealed so that dust particles do not corrupt it. The read/write head of the disk drive is able to move quickly over the surface of the disk, as it does not touch it directly, but is held just above it by air pressure. A megabyte is a million bytes. A 20Mb hard disk therefore can hold 20 million bytes of information.

360k byte floppy disk storage

A floppy disk is a thin disk, made of plastic, whose surface is covered in particles which can be magnetised. The disk is encased in a plastic wallet, the inside of which cleans the surface of the disk. Holes in the disk permit the read/write head to read or write data. A 360 kilobyte disk contains 360 x 1024 bytes of information. Floppy disks, unlike hard disks, can be removed from the drive which is used to contain them.

800 x 400 pixel high resolution graphics

A pixel (an abbreviation for pictorial element) is the basic element of graphical display on a computer screen (ie one of the dots which lights up to make a picture). Pixels vary in size, and so the number available that can fit into the size of a VDU screen is variable. High resolution graphics, are so called because a very large number of small pixels can be used to make a picture. The image is thus quite detailed. If graphics are described as low resolution, this means that each pixel is much bigger, and so the picture is more crude.

2 x RS232 asynchronous/synchronous ports

A port is a socket at the side of the microcomputer, to which various peripheral devices, either input or output can be attached. RS232 is a common serial interface. In the computer, all the bits in a byte are sent down a bus from one part of the computer to another in parallel (side-by-side), whereas some peripheral devices require the bits in a byte to be sent in series (ie one after the other). A serial interface, like RS232, converts the computer's parallel signals into serial ones, and vice versa. Synchronous transmission means that the bits are sent in regular time, controlled by the computer's clock. Asynchronous transmission is when each byte is preceded by a start bit and a stop bit.

1 parallel/IEEE port

This is a parallel interface, between a computer and peripheral devices.

20 HARDWARE FEATURES

> *Tutorial note.* This is a fairly straightforward question on hardware and offers an opportunity to score highly. The question asks for a diagram and so you will be penalised if you do not include one (or if your presentation is poor). You may have chosen to draw pictures of each device rather than a representational diagram as included here. If you did so, this is fine, but do not spend too long on creative artistry - just sketch enough to show the examiner that you know what you are talking about!

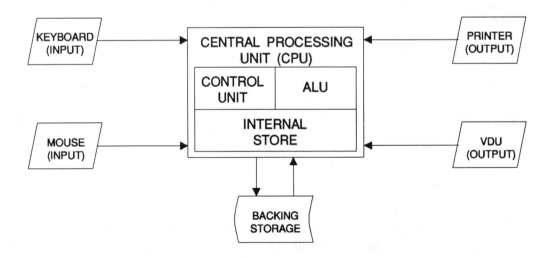

Keyboard. This is the most widely used means of input to a computer in typical business applications. The layout of a keyboard is based on the traditional QWERTY setting found on typewriters. There are also a number of additional keys, including a number pad (like a pocket calculator) to the right of the keyboard and a row of 'function' keys above the main keys. These function keys provide one-touch instructions when used in conjunction with many software packages.

Mouse. This is an input device which allows easy movement of the cursor around the screen; instead of positioning by means of arrow keys on the keyboard, the cursor responds to movement in any direction of the mouse, which senses motion by means of a roller fitted to its underside. The mouse also allows menu and option selection by means of depression of a button mounted on its surface.

Printer. This is used for output where hard copy is required. Printers generally offer printing on either A3 'computer paper', frequently used in accounting applications, or in A4 format, typically employed in word processing. Printers may be impact or non-impact.

VDU. The most commonly used form of output is the visual display unit. This is usually used in conjunction with a keyboard, and displays results of processing, current status of data entered or replies to enquiries on a screen resembling a small television screen. This means that the printer only needs to be employed once the user is satisfied with his work. Most computers offer a 'screen-print' facility, by which a print-out can be obtained of the screen display itself. VDUs may be colour or monochrome.

Backing storage. This includes not only an array of magnetic disks and tapes, but also a 'hard disk'. The hard disk is permanently mounted in a typical business microcomputer (although it can be removed for maintenance or repair purposes). Floppy disks may be in one of two formats, either 3½" or 5¼" and these can be inserted into and removed from disk drives as required. Tapes are not generally used with microcomputers because of the access times required, but are frequently used with minicomputers and mainframes.

Central Processing Units. The control unit supervises the execution of programs and coordinates the operation of peripheral (input and output) devices. The arithmetic and logic unit (ALU) carries out program instructions using appropriate operations such as arithmetical functions, comparisons, branches (to access individual parts of programs and read/write operations. The third part of the CPU is the internal memory, or main store. This is storage which is immediately accessible by the computer. (Data from backing storage must be retrieved and placed in internal memory before it can be processed.) The operating system software is held in internal memory, which also has a working areas for executing current programs.

21 HARDWARE DEVICES

Tutorial note. The least popular part of this question when it appeared in the exam was part (b). Laser printers have become very widespread in recent years as their prices have fallen. They now cost typically anything from £1,000 to £3,000. They do not use 'continuous stationery' but can be loaded with a tray of sheets of paper, rather like those used with a photocopier.

(a) *Mouse*

A mouse is usually part of the WIMP system (windows, icons, mouse, pull-down menu) which provides the operator a user-friendly interface to the computer. On screen can be found a number of words or icons (pictures) indicating a processing function to be performed. A pointer (or cursor) is used to select the desired option. When the option is selected the task will be executed, or further options, perhaps listed in a pulldown menu, are presented to the user.

The role of the mouse in this system is to enable the user to move the cursor anywhere round the screen in any direction. The mouse contains a rolling ball, and so can be moved over the top of the desk. As it does so, the cursor moves in a like direction on the screen. Once the option is reached, the user can execute it by depressing a small key on top of the mouse.

(b) *Laser printer*

Laser printers are based on photocopier technology. They print a whole page at a time, rather than line by line, on to individual sheets of paper. A laser printer works by means of a laser beam shining on to a photoconductive drum, and where the light strikes the drum, it becomes electrically charged. This then attracts toner which is fixed on to the paper by heat and pressure, to produce the printed page. The resolution of printed characters and diagrams with laser printers is very high - up to 600 dots per inch - and this high-quality resolution makes laser printing output good enough to be used for printing.

Laser printers are a microprocessor in their own right, with RAM memory for storing data prior to printing.

There are several distinct advantages of laser printers.

(i)   They can be used to combine different 'fonts' - eg italics, bold characters etc - and a wide range of characters, including mathematical symbols, Greek letters etc.

(ii) They can be used to produce graphics and logos as well as characters. A firm can therefore produce letter-heads as well as the letters themselves on to blank paper using a laser printer.

(iii) They are quiet, because unlike daisy wheel and dot matrix printers, laser printers are not 'impact' printers which rely on the striking of hammers or pins.

The cost of laser printers is higher than daisy wheel and dot matrix printers but, if local area networks develop sufficiently, it is quite possible that several terminals will opt to share a single laser printer.

(c) *Winchester disk*

A Winchester disk is a form of flying head disk (made from aluminium with a coating of magnetic material such as ferric oxide or chromium oxide). The read/write head on the disk unit is positioned extremely close to the disk, but not quite touching its surface. When the disk is revolving at high speed the read/write head is kept away from the disk surface by air pressure. This close positioning of the read/write head to the disk enables a flying head disk to operate much more quickly than other disk systems (eg. floppy disks).

A Winchester disk consists of one or more 'platters' and allows the head to land on the surface of the disk when it is not working, rather than to retract away. A special 'landing zone', which is not used for recording data, is provided on the outside track, and the head rests on this track when the disk is stationary. The speed of operating and the close proximity of the read/write head to the disk means that data can be packed very closely on the disk.

Winchester disks give a good recording density at a low cost, ie a high storage capacity per £1 cost. They are also quite small in physical size.

However, hard disks such as Winchester disks are fixed disks, and cannot be removed, so they do gradually fill up.

A possible disadvantage of high storage volumes is the security of 'dumping' data on file. The speed of dumping such a large file can be quite slow. Using a second hard disk for back-up is expensive, and so cheaper back-up storage media are used. It is now increasingly common to dump the contents of a Winchester disk on to magnetic tape cartridge, because this is quicker than dumping on to floppy disks.

To protect the disks physically, they must be kept free of airborne particles, and so each disk is encased in a hermetically-sealed container (and also with an efficient air filter).

Hard disks with a microcomputer might be:

(i) *external.* These sit alongside the computer in an extra 'box', with its own power supply and plug socket;

(ii) *internal.* These are incorporated inside the microcomputer itself. Internal hard disks tend to have less storage space than external disks.

(d) *Hi-resolution monitor*

A monitor is the name for the screen which forms part of the VDU. Most monitors employ the same technology as television, ie cathode ray tube. In some computers, especially portables and laptops, the visual display is provided by a different technology, for example gas plasma, or liquid crystal display.

A screen is made out of a number of dots called pixels (pictorial elements). The more pixels there are the greater the detail that can be displayed on screen. This is referred to as resolution. The degree of resolution and the number of colours on a monitor are expressed by the graphics standard. The standard is expressed mathematically as, for example 320 (horizontal) x 200 (vertical) pixels.

CGA was a common low-resolution standard now only sold on some laptops. The business standard is called EGA which offers a 640 x 350 resolution with 16 colours. A low-resolution monitor is say 320 x 200, whereas a high resolution monitor offers 1024 x 768.

The high-resolution monitors, especially those which offer a large palette of colours, require a great deal of memory (eg the VGA standard which offers 256 colours requires one byte per pixel) and so speed may be a casualty of the massively enhanced display.

High resolution display is required for the many graphics applications for computer-aided design applications and so forth.

(e) *Magnetic stripe reader*

A magnetic stripe reader is used in systems where data is input in part from a magnetic stripe on the back of a plastic card. The most common example is provided by the cards that are used in automated teller machines. The stripe will detail the customer's name, account number and some other details. With the input of the customer's PIN, the customer's account is accessed.

Magnetic stripe readers are also used in other commercial applications. Many shops which accept credit cards have a device connecting them over a network to the credit card company's central computer. As well as retailing, magnetic stripes are used in the telephone systems (BT's Phonecards, and Mercury's equivalent) and in public transport (for example the ticketing system on the London Underground railway).

22 BASIC REVISION QUESTION: INPUT AND OUTPUT

(a) *Input*

    (i)   On a microcomputer, input is usually by means of a keyboard. The operator checks the data as he or she inputs it, by looking at a 'visual display unit' (VDU). Occasionally, a 'mouse' or a 'joystick' is used to direct the cursor on a VDU, particularly when input is in the form of a diagram or graph. Rarer methods of input are light pens and touch screens.

    (ii)   Output data, for a microcomputer, is usually shown on the VDU, or it is printed out as 'hard copy' by some sort of printer.

        (1)   Output displayed on a VDU can be in black and white (in fact, more often green background and black type), or in colour, and can be in the form of text, graph, diagram or picture. Output on the VDU is temporary.

        (2)   Output displayed as hard copy by a printer can be as varied as that on screen but has the additional feature of being permanent. For microcomputers, the two main types of printer used are *dot matrix* and *daisywheel*. Dot matrix printers are cheaper and more versatile, but daisywheel printers produce higher quality printed material.

(b) *Output*

Data storage means the way in which data or programs are held outside the computer, ready to be used by the computer at a later date. For a microcomputer, data storage is usually magnetic tape (more often cartridge than reel), or magnetic disk (more often 'floppy' than hard).

    (i)   Magnetic tape in cartridge form is similar to but larger in size than the normal audio cassette made for a cassette tape recorder. File organisation and the method of processing on cartridge is sequential. Therefore, they do not allow for immediate retrieval of data. This fact, coupled with considerable developments in direct access storage facilities, has led to a relative decline in the use of magnetic tape, even though the cost of storage (in characters per £) is generally lower on tape than on disk.

    (ii)   A *floppy* disk is an exchangeable, circular flexible disk (typically 8 inches, 5¼ inches or 3½ inches in diameter) which is held permanently in a square paper sleeve. Microcomputers also us *Winchester* disks, which are hard disks developed especially for smaller computers, and are typically 8" or 5¼" in diameter. Floppy disks are cheaper than Winchester disks, but have a smaller storage capacity and are less robust. Data on both kinds of disks is accessed directly and quickly.

23 BASIC REVISION QUESTION: DATA CAPTURE

Direct document reading involves the use of a source document that can be read by the computer, so removing the problems created by data transcription. There are various methods of producing documents that computers can read; they include magnetic ink character recognition (MICR), optical mark reading (OMR) and bar coding.

MICR used stylized characters printed in magnetic ink. This method is very accurate and is used by banks to read data from cheques. Bar coding uses data recorded in binary using a code of alternating lines and spaces. It is often used on food items in supermarkets.

A *turnround document* is a document that is initially produced by a computer. It is then used to collect more data and is then re-input to the computer for processing. This method improves the accuracy of data as it keeps transaction errors to a minimum. It increases the speed to data capture and is reasonably cheap to produce and use. The optical character recognition method (OCR) is used, for example, by credit companies. They include a payment counterfoil with the computer-produced bill which is then used for inputting payment data to a computer.

On-line data entry methods have been developed so that input can be fed directly into a computer using a keyboard. The user has a method of receiving a response from the system (often a VDU) so the computer user can get the information required quickly. Keyboard input is convenient for small volumes of data when the time taken up by data input is only short. Most micro-computer systems in offices use keyboard and VDU for data input. Car insurance firms, for instance, often use on line data entry to input customer details and give an immediate estimate.

24 DATA CAPTURE

Data can be captured in a number of ways, with varying degrees of automation.

(i) Traditional input media (eg punched cards) require the laborious conversion, by human beings, of source documents into a form suitable for the computer to read ('machine-sensible'). An example of this type of data capture is 'key-to-tape' methods where a human operative will type details of transactions on to magnetic tape for further processing. There was thus considerable scope for error. Data collected in this way is almost always batch processed.

(ii) To reduce the scope for error and to save time, various means were devised to permit the computer to read the source documents directly. These include:

(a) character recognition, where the computer, using special equipment is able to 'read' numbers and letters (characters) directly (eg optical character recognition, where a laser is used to read characters, or magnetic ink character recognition where characters are written in magnetic ink);

(b) mark recognition, where, for example, a preprinted form is filled in with a number of ticks or crosses in specified boxes, which are read by the computer.

In both methods the computer converts this information to machine code.

Turnround documents may be used. This is a document produced by computer, filled in or marked in some way, and then submitted to the computer for further processing.

(iii) Data can be captured directly as the transaction occurs. Methods (i) and (ii) above both involve a time lag between the transaction and its capture by the computer. An example of direct capture is the use of bar codes in supermarkets. This is a form of mark-recognition, but the details of a sale are captured as soon as it occurs. Again, special equipment is used.

(iv) Data capture can be 'interactive'. Interactive data capture normally is achieved through the keyboard and VDU method of input. The originator is made aware of the effects of the transaction as soon as it has been input. For example, an airline reservation system will require a customer booking to be captured and processed immediately. Output provided, over a VDU, will indicate what choice of seats is available, and, once a seat is chosen, the booking will be confirmed. Here, data capture is on-line and real-time, and the provision of output is essential to the process.

25 DATA ENTRY

> *Tutorial note.* This is a question where it is easy to go wrong if you do not read the requirements carefully. When it was set in the exam many candidates restricted their answers to an explanation of the difference between batch and real-time systems, and ignored the main issue of data capture methods.

Key to disk

Source data can be transcribed on to a magnetic disk from a keyboard by a process of encoding. A VDU might be used to give a visual check of the encoding process. Key to disk input can be:

● off-line, where special encoding equipment is used to write the data on to the hard disk;

● on-line, where a computer is used, but where the data is stored on disk before being processed.

Generally, key-to-disk encoding systems are multi-station systems comprising a number of keyboard/VDU terminals on-line to a small computer. In larger systems a supervisor who is responsible for the work of the data preparation staff, sits at a terminal from which he or she schedules the source data to be transcribed and controls the input and loading of it on to files. Magnetic disks or diskettes are used to hold the prepared data which is copied from the manual source documents by the keyboard operators at each work station.

The system is controlled by the system's mini- or microcomputer using a small library of programs. These are able to carry out some *validation checks* on the data as it is keyed in (each application will have its own program of validation checks), and also control the encoding and *verification* processes.

The verification procedure is as follows.

(a) An operator at one of the key-stations (terminals) identifies the batch number of the data and the key-station number. This gives the encoded data an identification number to distinguish it from other key-stations. Data is keyed in, validated and formulated on the VDU screen (detected errors are indicated on the screen) and when accepted, written on to the magnetic disk.

(b) *Verification* is carried out by another operator at any other key-station by changing its operation into the 'verifying mode'. The second keying in is compared to the data on the disk, and errors are indicated and corrected by the operator. The verified data is written back on to the disk. This should now be free of all keying-in errors.

(c) Completed batches are grouped together to create the complete transaction file which is written from the working disks to another disk (or possibly a magnetic tape). This disk is then used as the input for the computer application program on the main computer.

When key-to-disk encoding is done via the main computer, and so controlled by a program in the main computer, *data validation* checks on the input data will probably be more extensive than with off-line key-to-disk encoding systems, and so more data errors in transaction records can be identified and corrected at an earlier stage in the processing.

In view of the cost of installing separate key-to-disk equipment, keyboard to disk via the main computer has become more common in recent years, instead of off-line encoding.

Key-to-disk encoding is suitable for data input preparation in systems where large volumes of data are input for processing.

Visual display units

Real time processing is said to occur when a transaction is processed when it is input, and the output is communicated immediately to the user. So, for example, if you are booking a pair of cinema tickets over the phone, your booking will be processed immediately, so that the number and location of seats available to subsequent callers is correctly stated. (Airline reservation systems are a little more sophisticated as they involve deliberate overbooking in case of cancellations). In short, in real time systems, the computer and user communicate interactively.

A visual display unit is a ubiquitous feature of any computer installation, whether it be the display used by a microcomputer, or as part of a terminal connected to a minicomputer or mainframe.

The VDU displays text and graphics, and sometimes, depending on the resolution, quite detailed pictorial images. The first monitors were monochrome, but now colour monitors with a large and sophisticated palette of colours are becoming more common. They do require, however, a considerable amount of processing power, so are only suitable for the more powerful machines now available. The screen is divided into dots (pixels, or pictorial elements): the more dots there are, the sharper the image. As graphic user interfaces become more widely available, the ability of a monitor to deliver high quality graphics in real time processing operations might become more important.

26 DIRECT DOCUMENT READING

Tutorial notes. 1. You were only required to describe *one* of the techniques outlined below. This was quite an unusual question, requiring quite a depth of knowledge about an individual item of hardware. 2. The model answers give actual examples of OCR and MICR fonts. You would not be expected to draw them in an exam!

All the methods mentioned are examples of direct document readers. A computer is able to read marks or characters made in predetermined positions on special forms, without the need for human transcription of data. Thus, it is hoped, that input errors, are reduced.

(a) *Mark sensing*

Mark sensing is a method of direct document reading that is now rather out of date, having been replaced by optical mark recognition (OMR). It was, however, one of the first methods of direct data input.

A card would be printed with predetermined positions outlined on it, to represent digits or characters. The user would make a mark, with a soft graphite pencil, at the desired points on the card. Using a pencil to make the mark was important, the reason being that graphite conducts electricity. The marks were read by passing an electric current through electric contacts which were 'brushed' over the card.

This is quite unlike optical mark reading (OCR) where the marks can be made in ballpoint, ink, or whatever, as they are read by reflected light.

Mark sensing was sometimes used to make punched cards, as a hole would be punched where the mark had been made. Like OMR, it can also be used to mark multiple choice examination questions, or to carry out other similar functions.

The diagram below indicates a card marked up for mark sensing, with the number 081.

	1	2	3	4	5	6	7	8	9
0	1	2	3	4	5	6	7		9
0		2	3	4	5	6	7	8	9

(b) *Optical character recognition*

Optical character recognition is a means of data input by which a machine is able to read characters by optical detection of the shape of those characters. This is obviously more sophisticated than optical mark reading.

An OCR reader uses light sensing to read stylised characters. These may be printed, or typed, for example.

Optical (or laser) scanners can recognise the characters, convert them into machine code and record them on to the input medium being used, or directly input the data to the CPU. Most machines still require particular typefaces, examples of which are OCR - A and OCR - B (ECMA 11):

```
OCR-A
ABCDEFGHIJKLMNOPQRSTUVWXYZ
1234567890:;⌠=⌐?"$%|&'{}*+¬-./▮⌑
OCR-B
ABCDEFGHIJKLMNOPQRSTUVWXYZ
1234567890|*-=+,./<>▮
```

Some OCR readers can read ordinary typed or printed text, provided that the quality of the input document is satisfactory. (Note: this is why banks cannot use OCR for cheques. Cheques would often be too crumpled for reading by OCR methods.)

Banks use OCR for processing *credits* between companies. Account/reference details can be printed on a bank giro credit slip.

(i)   The OCR equipment shines a light on to the coded line.
(ii) Each character is projected on to a screen containing 96 photo-electric sensors.
(iii) The reader determines the voltage of each element thus understanding the character.

(c)   *Magnetic ink character recognition (MICR)*

Using ink which contains a metallic powder (ferric oxide), highly stylised characters are encoded on to documents by means of special typewriters.

MICR works in the following way.

(i)   Each cheque has MICR characters at the bottom indicating:

   1.   the cheque's serial number;
   2.   the bank and branch code;
   3.   the customer's account number.

   This is *pre-encoded information.*

(ii) Cheques are sent to the clearing centre, and are exchanged between banks.

   The details written on the cheque (eg the amount) are *post-encoded* underneath the handwritten details, for processing.

(iii) The banks process the cheques by passing each cheque through a MICR reader/sorter.

   1.   A write head magnetises the character.
   2.   A read head reads the magnetic signal. The shape of the electronic signal corresponds to the strength of the magnetic field.

(iv) The computer analyses the signal shape, and so data is input.

Up to 2,000 documents can be scanned each minute.

MICR requires the use of special typefaces, the most common of which are E 13B used by the British and American banks, and CMC 7 used in Europe. An example of each is shown below.

1 8

ENLARGED

1234567890 ⑈⑆⑇⑈

ACTUAL SIZE
E 13 B FOUNT

ENLARGED

⑆⑈⑇⑈⑆⑇1234567890

ABCDEFGHIJKLMNOPQRSTUVWXYZ

ACTUAL SIZE
C.M.C. 7 FOUNT

27 BASIC REVISION QUESTION: POINT OF SALE TERMINALS

(a) Four benefits of installing point-of-sale devices are:

(i) the computer will be able to produce management information quickly (eg sales details and analysis);

(ii) the computer can monitor stock levels and institute re-order procedures as soon as it becomes necessary;

(iii) the computer will look up product prices and produce the final cost to the customer, eliminating work which used to be carried out by the cashier, and so reducing errors;

(iv) customers should pass more quickly through the checkouts.

(b) In order to achieve the point-of-sales plan, Cans and Co will need:

(i) a stock file, with a record for each item, which will indicate stocks currently held, re-order level and cost price;

(ii) a suppliers file, which gives details of suppliers when it becomes necessary to re-order items;

(iii) a price file, which would be a master file containing the prices of all items;

(iv) a sales file, which records the sales details over a length of period. The exact detail held on the sales file will vary according to the precise information required by Cans and Co.

28 EPOS

> *Tutorial note.* Although EPOS is a relatively new application of information technology, it has been around for some years and the examiner is certainly justified in expecting you to be able to tackle a question like this, which emphasises the importance of keeping up to date with the subject. Note carefully the mark split; it is clear that you should not have spent too long on part (a), otherwise you would have reduced your scoring potential in part (b).

(a)   In a typical EPOS system, the retailer's cash register is replaced by a computer terminal which retains the features of a cash till, but includes an electronic link to the retailer's computer and incorporates one of a number of sophisticated input devices. Goods in the store are all coded with a unique (to each item) bar code. For each code used, a master file on the store's computer holds the selling price per item and other relevant data (eg discounts for multiple purchases of an item). When a customer presents goods for purchase, the cashier or checkout operator 'reads' the bar code, either with a light pen drawn across the code or by means of passing the item over an electronic eye so that the code is presented to the resulting beam. The code data is transmitted electronically to the computer, which transmits the selling price, and a product description for automatic inclusion on the customer's receipt. The computer updates stock and sales accounting records at the same time.

EPOS systems greatly reduce human error in inputting data, as well as improving checkout efficiency and productivity. Stock control is improved and it is also likely that customer fraud (eg by substituting lower price labels which are subsequently read and input by the cashier) is reduced.

(b)   EPOS systems provide a wide range of information which can be used to support the decision making process.

   (i)   *Stock usage.* An EPOS system can give details of fast-moving and slow-moving stock lines. This is particularly important for food retailers where many types of goods have a very short shelf-life. Decisions can be made to discount slow-moving items to promote sales.

   (ii)   *Stock re-ordering.* EPOS systems can be programmed to generate stock orders when stock reaches a certain level. These can be accepted and used, or overridden.

   (iii)   *Sales analyses.* EPOS systems can provide extremely detailed sales analyses, so that the effect of promotions and discounts can be analysed. Decisions can be made on whether or not to continue stocking certain items and whether to increase or reduce the shelf space allocated to others.

   (iv)   *Customer behaviour.* The data held on an EPOS system can be used to provide information on shopping habits, eg size of purchases, number of customers, peak periods in shopping week etc. Decisions can be made on temporary staffing requirements, appropriate times for staff training, and best patterns for shift arrangements.

29 BASIC REVISION QUESTION: PRINTERS

(a) *Daisy wheel*

Daisy wheel printers are quite widely used in microcomputer systems. A metal or plastic print wheel is used, which may be changed to alter character styles, and which can normally print 96 different characters. The characters, arranged on the wheel circumference on 'spokes', strike the paper through a carbon ribbon and bold lettering is achieved by a slightly offset second strike. Printing speeds vary from 15-55 characters per second. These speeds are relatively slow but this type of printer is primarily used where print quality is more important than speed.

(b) *Dot matrix*

These are the most commonly used printers in microcomputer systems. A set of small pins is arranged in a vertical matrix. The matrix moves along the line of paper to print each character, which is individually shaped by selected pins being pressed onto the paper through an inked ribbon. The main advantages are the greater speed of printing, up to 400 characters per second, and the fact that character styles are under software control, allowing a greater variety of character styles. The disadvantages of dot matrix printers is that print quality is not as high as with character impact printers. Such printers are used where volumes are high and speed is important.

(c) *Thermal*

Thermal printers are lightweight printers which use special heat sensitive paper. The printer creates heat that in turn produces printed output on the special paper. Thermal printers are cheap but the paper is expensive. They are particularly useful as portable devices because of their light weight, especially where the quantity of print out is low, thus limiting the cost of the paper.

30 COMPUTER OUTPUT

> *Tutorial note.* This was the third time that the examiner tested candidates' knowledge of the term 'high resolution' in the space of two years. In spite of this, he wrote that few understood the reasons for the term or its importance in particular applications.

(a) *Computer output on microform (COM)*

COM is a form of computer output whereby instead of printing the output on to paper, it is projected on to a cathode ray tube and then photographed into a very much reduced form - ie into a microform. (Alternative methods of producing COM involve laser beam, electron beam or optical fibre technology.)

The microform is readable, but not to the unassisted naked eye, and a magnifying reading device (with a viewing screen) is needed by users. To assist the user in finding the records on the microform, 'eyeball' characters - ie letters or numbers visible to the eye without magnification - are created on the microform.

- *Microfilm* is a continuous strip, with images formed in frames one at a time all along the strip of the film.

- *Microfiche* on the other hand, consist of separate sheets of film (at least three times wider than microfilm) each sheet containing over 100 frames or 'pages' of information.

When microform is produced by computer, it may be produced either on-line or off-line. When it is produced on-line there is a microform-producing peripheral device on-line to the CPU, whereas off-line production involves producing a magnetic tape (or disk) by the CPU and using the tape as input to an off-line microform-producer.

Both systems have the following advantages over printer output.

(i) *Large volumes of information can be condensed* into a very small physical space so that savings in storage space can be considerable where printed matter would otherwise have to be kept for fairly long periods of time.

(ii) Microform therefore provides a suitable storage medium for *archive information* or reference information.

(iii) Microform frames or *pages can be reproduced on paper* in an enlarged, readable form, if required.

Microform has the *disadvantage* of needing *special reading devices*, so that if the output is in regular use by various staff in a department, there might be 'bottleneck' problems for them in getting access to the information they need, as they queue up to use the reading device.

(b) *Graph plotters*

Graph plotters are output devices which use a variety of coloured pens to draw and also shade graphs and charts on paper. With the growing use of graphics packages they are becoming more popular. Also, packages such as spreadsheets contain graphics facilities, and the use of a graph plotter enables printed output of much higher quality to be produced.

Graph plotters come in two broad types.

The flat bed graph plotter is one in which a the paper is put in a frame. Two split metal bars perpendicular to each other move in a horizontal plane from left to right and from top to bottom, thus moving the pen attached at their intersection of the two bars.

A drum plotter is one in which the paper is attached to the drum. While the pen moves in one plane, the paper moves in another.

(c) *High resolution monitor*

A VDU screen (or *monitor*) displays text and graphics. In the past there was only a limited of data (24 lines x 80 columns) that could be displayed on screen at any particular time. However, monitors are now capable of supporting colour and detailed display. Monitors are either cathode ray tubs, liquid crystal displays or gas plasma display.

Some graphics software packages provide the following facilities.

(i) The use of different *colours*. These are achieved either by specifying, from a fairly limited selection on offer, or, in advanced graphics packages from mixing or matching the desired colours from a palette. ArtWorks paint offers in theory 16 million colours.

(ii)   *Multi-level masking*. This facility enables images to be superimposed on each other, with the image behind still visible.

(iii)   *Colour cycling*. Colours can be animated to suggest movement such as water flowing through a pipe.

(iv)   *Video feed*. Some packages will enable picture fed from a video to be displayed on screen, with computer graphics at the same time.

(v)   The stages of image creation can be saved and replayed *as a sequence*.

(vi)   Images can be drawn, freehand, using a mouse. Alternatively, some packages offer stencils to help you draw. A 'rubberband' feature might be presented, which means that circles or ovals can be pulled to the required shape.

(vii)   A package might be able to generate, automatically, three dimensional graphs, with shading.

The screen's *resolution* is the number of pixels that are lit up. A pixel is a pictorial element - a 'dot' on the screen, as it were. A program can instruct the VDU screen to light up a pixel on any x and y coordinate and this is how computer graphics are formed on a screen. The fewer the pixels on screen, the larger they will be: the resolution of any picture will be low. More and smaller pixels enable detailed high-resolution display. High resolution monitors currently available include 1024 (horizontal) x 768 (vertical). Currently, many PCs have a resolution of 640 x 480. (This is the resolution offered by IBM's VGA standard.) Higher resolution requires more processing power.

(d)   *Daisy wheel printers*

In a daisy wheel printer, fully formed print characters are positioned at the end of long stems, which protrude from a central wheel. This gives the impression of a daisy-like flower, with a solid round centre and petals sticking out all around it - hence the name of the printer.

The daisy wheel is inserted in the printer, and rotates until the desired character is in the right position. A hammer then strikes the end of the stem and the character appears on the paper.

Daisy wheels can be changed, if a different font is required (eg italics) but only one daisy wheel can be used at a time.

Print speeds can range from 10 to 80 characters per second, depending on the make and quality of printer.

The constant hammering of characters against paper make daisy wheel printers very noisy, which can be a serious drawback in an office environment, where hard-copy output is required in large amounts.

The advantage of daisy wheel printers is their ability to print fully-formed characters and so produce letter-quality output. Daisy wheels were the main type of printer used with office word processor systems, until the advent of laser printers, and the increasing use of computer graphics and desk-top publishing systems.

31 DISKS AND TAPES

(a) (i) Magnetic tape is a continuous medium and therefore file organisation must either be serial (ie, records are processed in the order in which they were recorded), or sequential (in which records are recorded in key field sequence).

File access is also serial or sequential; direct access, indexed sequential access and random access with an index are not possible with magnetic tape.

To update a record on magnetic tape, the record firstly has to be read from the tape into the CPU. Thus the updated record cannot be written back to the same physical place on the tape (because the tape has 'wound forward' beyond that point). Therefore to update a record on a magnetic tape, a new tape file is created with a copy of all the unchanged data and with the addition of the updated records.

(ii) Magnetic disks are very versatile and in addition to serial and sequential file organisation (as described for magnetic tapes), record organisation on a disk may be indexed sequential (where records are filed sequentially with an index used to locate individual files), or random (where records have no sequential order).

File access on magnetic disks may be serial or sequential (as for magnetic tape) but may also be direct where any record can be accessed without first reading all the earlier records.

An indexed sequential file on disk can be processed in several ways.

1. *Sequential*, as for magnetic tapes. This is used where the hit rate is high.

2. *Selective sequential*, where only records requiring updating are read and processed.

3. *Random*, where the index is used to locate a particular record for updating and the read/write heads move directly to that record. This method is used when the hit rate is low.

Direct access is used for randomly organised files where the hit rate is low, a fast response is required or data cannot be conveniently batched or sorted. Random organisation is commonly used in real time systems.

A sequentially organised disc can be updated by file copying (as with magnetic tape) but file overlay is usually used, as for randomly organised disk. In this method the updated record is written directly back to its original location address on the disk.

(b) Magnetic tapes are often used to back up disk files as they have the advantage of higher storage capacity and are generally cheaper. Tape is a generally safer and more robust medium than disks for storage. Fast tapes called tape streamers have been developed for back up purposes. If the hit rate is high, magnetic tape may still be faster than processing by disk and some large bulk processing commercial systems would prefer tape over disk. Tapes may also be used for a payroll master file where the processing is batch mode.

Magnetic disks are much more versatile in their methods of file access and are now the main medium for file storage. If information is needed quickly, or if the user requires information and needs to update the data at the same time, then direct access is necessary. Direct access (ie magnetic disk) is also needed to operate in real time, when files are required to be up-to-date. Magnetic disks would be used, for example, in banks, as the data is continually being updated and information is required quickly.

32 BATCH AND REAL-TIME PROCESSING

Tutorial note. The examples of each type of processing given below are fairly standard. A payroll run can be subjected to batch processing - the only constraint is that it must be completed by the time it is necessary to make up pay packets and send credit transfer details to the bank. Batch processing is not suitable for airline reservations - just imagine what would happen if all bookings were recorded on input forms and then put in a pile for processing at the end of the week!

Batch processing can be defined as the 'processing as a group of a number of transactions of a similar kind which have been entered over a period of time to a computer system.' (CIMA Computing Terminology)

Real-time processing can be defined as 'the continual receiving and rapid processing of data so as to be able, more or less instantly, to feed back the results of that input to the source of that data.' (CIMA Computing Terminology)

Real-time processing occurs on demand, and the results of real-time processing are known instantaneously. Information produced by a real-time system by definition is always up-to-date. A batch processing system does not produce up-to-date information. The grouping of transactions means that there is a delay in their being processed.

Batch processing example

Batch processing is used to process groups of routine transactions, and there are many example where it can be used. One example could be provided by a payroll system.

Payroll is a good example of the appropriateness of a batch processing operation. Its functions are relatively self-contained in that there is only a limited input to other systems. The output required is predictable and regular: the payment dates of wages and salaries, whether weekly or monthly, are set in advance. Input, also, is easy to assess: the pay for hourly paid workers will be determined in part by timesheets. For salaried employees, basic pay is determined over longer time periods, adjustments being, for example, annual, whereas overtime details are likely to be input each time the payroll is run. Other factors affecting the payroll include the recording of bonus payments, sales commission, tax and National Insurance rates, starters and leavers.

A batch processing payroll application would work in the following way. Timesheets would be sent in by the appropriate departments, and these are coded on a special input form. The coded details are batched together and may be transcribed on to magnetic tape before input. The data is then input, subjected to any data validation checks and processed. Records may need to be sorted into the sequence of records on the payroll master file, which are probably held in employee number order. Output takes the from of salary slips and perhaps a magnetic tape to be used for the direct transfer of funds from the employer's to employees' bank accounts. Other output could include wages cost by department, overtime analysis and so forth.

The processing run is not likely to take more than a few hours. In the periods between payroll runs, up-to-date information could not be provided by the computer, and the wages owed to leavers for example would be determined manually.

As processing and file access is sequential the hardware used could be a magnetic tape system.

Real-time processing example

An example of a real-time processing system is provided by an airline reservation and ticketing system.

The British Airways Booking System (BABS), which is operated by a central computer at Heathrow linked to British Airways agents in the UK, Europe, USA, South America, Australia etc via a communications network (telephone and satellite). An intending passenger may enquire at an airline office or travel agents for a flight to a particular place on a certain day. The reservation clerk is able to ascertain immediately if there is a vacancy, and then make a booking if required to do so. If no seats are available the computer will indicate possible alternatives for the customer's consideration (a travel agent will have access to many airlines' flight details). This is a good example of a real-time system in that the response to the original enquiry is received sufficiently quickly for the customer to await it, and make a decision based on that response. As well as maintaining all the passenger lists and flight information details the system allows highly specific enquiries to be made, (eg a passenger list of all families with children under 2 years old flying first class from London to New York on 4 July whose surname begins with H or L), the computer system as a whole as to handle flight control, plan air-crew scheduling, and perform the various other accounting and routine applications.

33 DATA STORAGE ON DISK

> *Tutorial note.* When this was set as an exam question, a large number of candidates wrote about different types of disk, rather than about data storage. This resulted in them earning few or no marks.

There are four options (including two sequential alternatives) for the organisation of data records on disk. One of the key factors influencing the approach adopted is the *hit rate*. This is the percentage of records on the master file which, on average, will be processed during a routine update.

On a magnetic disk, file access may be serial or sequential, as for magnetic tape. However, disk offers a third possibility: *direct* access. This is rather like one of the advantages that compact disc offers over audiocassette when listening to music; any track on the compact disc can be selected almost instantaneously, or directly, while a tape must be spooled to the appropriate point in order to 'read', or play, a particular track. A CD can of course be played through from beginning to end, just as a computer disk can be processed from start to finish.

(i) *Serial organisation.* This is the storage of records in the order in which they are input. Serial organisation is only used for temporary files, eg transaction files. When contents of a master file which is being updated are *dumped* (for security purposes), these might also be stored serially.

(ii) *Sequential organisation.* This method is appropriate where the hit rate is high. If an index were used and each record accessed directly, processing would be extremely slow where most records on the master file required updating.

Sequential organisation involves the holding of records in *key field* sequence, for example by account number. This means that the first transaction record, eg 0003 is taken and the master file is searched sequentially, through 0001 and 0002 until 0003 is found. This record can then be updated. The next transaction record is then taken, eg 0005, and the master file search continues from 0003, rather than having to return to 0001, as the records are in key field order.

Since new records may not be of the same length as those they are replacing, this approach requires a complete over-writing of the masterfile, as otherwise overlaps would occur and records would be partially deleted. Therefore if only a small number of records are to be updated, ie the hit rate is low, it is not very efficient. An example of an application where every record is updated every period is payroll.

(iii) *Indexed sequential organisation.* Under this method, records continue to be held in key field sequence, but an index is held on disk to enable direct access. If a master file is organised indexed sequentially, it does not matter whether a transaction file is organised sequentially or not, as access is equally quick in either case. Index sequential organisation requires spaces between records, so that if a new record is longer, it can either be inserted into the space or failing that a marker inserted and the excess written to an overflow area on the disk.

(iv) *Random organisation.* Records may be organised in any sequence under random organisation. An index is used; this is generated by means of establishing some kind of link between the record's address on file and its key field. Thus records which are preceded by a particular digit may be stored in a particular sector or block of the disk. Random organisation is suitable where the hit rate is low or where a fast response is necessary. It is used in real time systems where there is no pattern to the sequence of enquiries or bookings and there is no time to wait while all records on the master file are sequentially read.

34 BASIC REVISION QUESTION: TELECOMMUNICATIONS TERMS

(a) Private automatic branch exchanges (PABX systems) provide facilities for office switchboards and telephone systems. These computerised (electronic or digital) exchanges can offer facilities such as automatic message switching, automatic dialling, conference calls or, when a line is engaged, call repeating.

(b) A packet switching systems (PSS) allows a number of computers to transmit data to each other in a more economical way than dedicated private lines. The data message in a PSS is divided up into packets which includes the identification of the sender and the address of its destination. Each computer in the PSS receives and redirects these packets along the network until it reaches its destination. It is then reassembled into the full message and transmitted to the recipient.

(c) Baud rate is a term used to mean bits per second transmitted. Data is usually transmitted by means of bit serial transmission where the bits that make up a character are sent down the line in turn. Alternatively there is bit parallel transmission which uses eight lines for an eight bit character where all bits are sent simultaneously.

35 DATA COMMUNICATION TERMS

> *Tutorial note.* Unlike many terminology-based questions, this one was quite restricted in the area examined, probing the depth of your knowledge rather than its breadth. You could not answered this question successfully without a clear awareness of the distinction between the various items of equipment noted. Knowing that they are something to do with data transmission is not enough.

(a) *Acoustic coupler*

An acoustic coupler is a form of *modem*. A modem is a device which is used in the transmission of data between computers over the telecommunications network. Modems are described in the suggested solution to part (c) of this question.

An acoustic coupler is a type of modem whereby the connection between the computer and the telecommunications network is made by a small microphone and loudspeaker connected to the computer held close to the mouthpiece and earpiece of a telephone handset. The computer's signals are converted into sound, sent via the loudspeaker to be picked up the by telephone's mouthpiece. It is then transmitted over the network. Messages received are transmitted as sound over the earpiece of the phone, and are picked up by the microphone.

Note that there is no electronic connection between the computer and the telecommunications network. The acoustic coupler will translate the data into analog form and back again. (See answer to part (c)).

(b) *Multiplexor*

A multiplexor is used to link several computers, terminals or other items of hardware to a single data link. Data is transmitted via a multiplexor at the other end of the link to other computers. A multiplexor is useful because a data link between, say, one terminal and one central processor would be idle most of the time: the messages travel much faster than humans can type them. This idle time can be used by another set of equipment. As it costs a great deal of money to lease telephone line, multiplexing, by enabling a link to be shared, ensures that they are used most productively.

There are two types of multiplexing. Time division multiplexing allocates particular time intervals to the various items of equipment. Frequency division multiplexing allocates different bandwidths to the various items of equipment.

(c) *Modem*

A modem is an item of equipment which enables computers and other equipment to communicate over the telecommunications link.

Most computers handle data in digital (bit) form. That is, the data is dealt with in discrete units, represented by the binary digits 0 and 1. Much of the telecommunications network uses analog transmission, whereby data is transmitted in wave form. The distinction can be represented by a wristwatch: a digital wrist watch displays the changing minutes by flashing numbers; an analog wrist watch measures time by the slow progression of the hand around the face.

The data in bit form from the computer has to be converted (modulated) into analog form before it is sent over the data link. At the other end of the link, another modem will convert it back again (demodulate) to digital form.

(d) *Asynchronous*

Asynchronous and synchronous transmission are two alternative ways of transmitting data.

With asynchronous transmission, one character is sent at a time over the link, and each character is preceded by a start bit, and followed by a stop bit. The receiving device recognises the start bit and reads the bits which follow until it comes to the stop bit. Microcomputers normally use asynchronous transmission. It is less efficient if very large volumes of data are to be transmitted at high speed, where synchronous transmission is more appropriate. In this case, the rate of transmission is determined by the computer's internal clock: if there are so many bits per time unit, and if for the purposes of argument the bits are of the same length, the time interval should be enough to determined when a character begins or ends.

(e) *Protocol*

A protocol is a 'defined set of rules which, if adhered to, ensure the correct interchange of data between two pieces of equipment.' A protocol is used to enable errors in data transmission (eg loss, wrong sequence) to be discovered. Also, a protocol might be able to identify which of the data transmitted was faulty.

There are many factors in the successful operation of a data link, from the purely physical connection, the proper use of the data link (messages sent and received in the right order), procedures for opening and closing communication links between computers and so forth. The International Standards Organisation has established a seven layer reference model for these factors, dividing the link into seven layers. This is a form of protocol.

Tutorial note. This diagram should enable you to picture the relationships between the items of equipment.

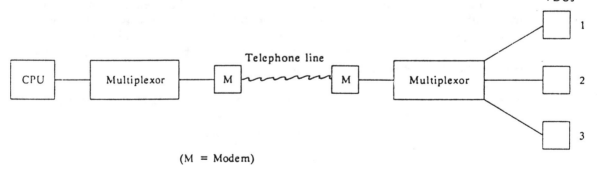

(M = Modem)

36 NETWORKS

(a) A local area network (LAN) is a means of interconnecting a modest number of machines (2 - 20, but sometimes more) over a small area (typically within a few hundred metres). Several sorts of networks exist, giving a variety of speed/cost/capacity trade-offs; essentially the faster the data transfer round the network, the more expensive the system.

Basically, the system consists of:

(i) a central disk file and program store, controlled by a 'server computer' usually a dedicated microcomputer called a control microcomputer;

(ii) a cable or 'data highway' linking this control microcomputer to the other micro-computers (or other devices):

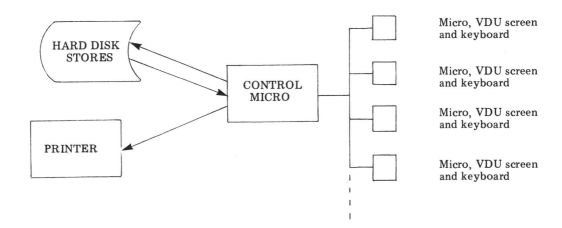

Extra micros can be 'plugged in' to the system. LANs are structured in a number of different ways and need special software to work properly.

The operation of a LAN is described below.

(i)   The 'remote' microcomputers load the application programs they require to use by calling them from the central store of programs. They also call up any data files required.

(ii)   All processing and input of transaction data is done at the remote micro. This leaves the central control micro and file store free to service other users.

(iii) When the remote micro has done its processing, the updated data is written back into the central store.

A wide area network (WAN) is similar to a LAN in concept, but is distinguished by:

(i)   being widely dispersed geographically;
(ii)   requiring a much larger 'server computer';
(iii) the use of the public telecommunications network.

A WAN is likely to require the use of modems.

A modem is used to convert (modulate) the bit form data into wave form data for transmission on public or private telephone lines. When the signal arrives the wave form must be de-modulated into bit form. Modem is short for 'modulator/demodulator' and it may be built into a special telephone for link-up with the remote computer, or it may take the form of an acoustic coupler. A multiplexor allows several users to send data down the line at one time. It codes data in a special way to allow sorting when it reaches its destination.

(b) Office work is mainly concerned with the processing, handling, storing and communication of information.

Typical office procedures include record maintenance, the arrangement of meetings, preparation and distribution of mail and memoranda.

LANs and WANs provide a means of automating office communication and information handling. The 'electronic office' can be recognised by:

(i)   a 'workstation' (terminal, VDU and keyboard) on every desk, linked over a LAN to other workstations, and perhaps to a central computer;

(ii)   the use of electronic Private Automatic Branch Exchanges;

(iii)   possible computer links to external suppliers of data, and/or, over a WAN, to other offices.

LANs permit:

(i)   direct workstation to workstation communication, which can take the form of electronic mail (E-mail);

(ii)   direct transmission of data from machine to machine (eg a spreadsheet prepared on one machine can be sent to another without the need to copy it onto a floppy disk and then reload it);

(iii)   data storage in one location so that duplication is no longer necessary;

(iv)   diary software which can automatically coordinate meeting times for busy executives;

(v)   in some electronic offices, with compatible software, data prepared on a spreadsheet to be sent to a word processor to improve the presentation.

Linkage to a WAN permits:

(i)   direct communication with other offices, broadly similar to the type of communication within the office;

(ii)   direct communication between suppliers and customers, whereby a customer need only input the other into the WAN, and the supplier's order book is updated immediately;

(iii)   access to third party databases (eg Prestel).

37 XAB LTD

(a)   *Distributed data processing* refers to a computer system which consists of many processors and items of peripheral equipment, all linked together in some form of communications network. Such a system allows processing to be carried out at several different locations, possibly over a wide geographical area. In particular, one computer can access the files of other computers in the system, and computers within the system may process data jointly ('interactively').

(b)   The features of a mini-computer in general are that:

(i)   unlike a mainframe computer, it does not need an air-conditioned environment in which to operate;

(ii)   it is relatively small (ie takes up little space) and its power requirements are modest;

(iii) users do not need to be highly trained;

(iv) software packages and add-on peripherals are readily available for most mini-computers.

If a mini-computer is set up as part of a distributed network, it will in addition:

(v) be able to access files in all other computers within the network (and its files will be available to the other computers);

(vi) be able to work jointly (interactively) with other computers in the network.

(c) *Tutorial note*: this part of the question is slightly ambiguous in that it could be asking for four types of distributed processing systems, or for four systems which could be processed through a distributed system. The latter interpretation has been taken for this answer, as it makes some use of the information given in the question about XAB Ltd.

(i) Sales order/sales analysis.

(ii) Stock control.

(iii) Invoicing/credit checking.

(iv) Purchasing.

38 MM ENTERPRISES

> *Tutorial note.* This question can be understood in a number of ways and there is not necessarily a 'right' answer. You should however learn to identify the main issues and develop a coherently justified solution. In this question, we are told that telecommunication methods are too expensive and paper is too bulky. Presumably this means that it is a difficult operation to phone each branch individually from head office. If information distribution is decentralised, as suggested below, the use of telecommunications is almost certainly the cheapest option.

(a) To determine an efficient and cost-effective means of transmitting data, we must identify the characteristics of the information and the circumstances of its distribution.

Characteristics of the data to be distributed

The information is bulky. Exactly the same information is sent to each branch, so the data has to be copied 300 times. We do not know whether the data is going to be input into the branch's own systems, in addition to the data processing carried out at group level.

Circumstances of distribution

The information is distributed to 300 branches, scattered over the world. Distribution is regular and frequent, as the information is sent to each branch *every week*.

It follows that given the above constraints, any medium for holding this data, must allow:

- rapid preparation, as data is distributed every week;

- rapid reproduction, as 300 copies are to be made of the same data;

- condensation to save carriage space, or telephonic distribution time;

- inexpensive transmission or distribution over the world.

There are a variety of available media.

- Paper has been ruled out as too bulky.

- Microfilm or microfiche can be prepared by photocopying hard-copy output, or can be originated directly by the computer. When 300 copies are needed, microfiching and microfilming are expensive and time-consuming.

- Magnetic media, such as a 'floppy disk', magnetic tape, either as a reel or as a cassette could be used, as all are portable.

All these methods involve the manual transportation to many different locations in the world. The following problems can be identified:

- expensive air fare and courier costs;

- time delays caused by airline timetables, customs inspections, inefficiencies in postal services;

- security against theft, loss or damage may require 'back-up' copies to be sent by alternative routes.

Although telecommunication links from UK head office to each individual branch have been ruled out as too expensive, there is a case for using telecommunication links between UK head office and a key branch in each geographical area where the company has a presence.

The advantage is that data transmission from the UK to, say, Asia would be practically instantaneous. Each key branch would then distribute data to other branches in the area.

(b) The UK head office and each of the key branches would possess a *modem* to permit the data to be sent and received over the telephone line. A modem (or modulator/demodulator) is needed because a computer stores and uses data in digital ('bit') form, but data is sent over a telephone line in analogue (or wave) form. The modem translates 'bit' form into 'wave' form and vice versa. The data once received would be called up on a *VDU*. It would be printed, if the data is to be distributed in hard copy format, and so a *printer* and photocopier would be necessary. Alternatively, the data could be copied on to a number of floppy diskettes for distribution.

A microcomputer attached to the modem with VDU and printer would seem an appropriate set up in the relevant branches.

39   IT TERMS

(a)   *Electronic mail*

Electronic mail is the transmission of data electronically, whereby the recipient does not have to receive the data immediately. Instead, the data can be stored in an electronic 'mail box' until the recipient wishes to collect any messages. Examples of electronic mail systems are Telecom Gold, and some of the data transmission facilities available through Prestel (viewdata).

(i)   The sender prepares his information on a microcomputer and transmits the message via the telephone network to a central mailbox. This is a part of a large BT computer's information store, which is assigned to the Telecom Gold subscriber.

(ii)   The subscriber picks up any message in his mailbox using another microcomputer and his telephone.

(b)   *Facsimile transmission*

Facsimile is the transmission of an exact copy of a document electronically, so that a duplicate can be produced at the recipient's end of the line of a facsimile machine. In effect, it is long distance photocopying.

40   SOFTWARE TERMINOLOGY

(a)   *Source program*

Any program written in a programming language is called a source program. It has to be translated into 'machine code' for the computer to understand it, and the machine code version of the program is called the 'object program'.

Machine code is comprised of binary digits, having the values 1 or 0. Machine code is specific to an individual make of machine. A piece of machine code normally specifies the address where an item of data can be found, and the operation that must be performed.

Languages were developed so that programmers need not work in binary. Assembly languages (low level languages) involve simple abbreviations, in symbolic form, of machine code (eg ADD). A program written in assembly language correlates directly with the machine code. An assembler program is used to translate from the assembly language source program machine code object program. An assembly language is machine-dependent.

Most source programs are originally written in a 'high level' language, like BASIC. There is no direct correlation between the high level language source program and the machine code object program, and high level languages are not restricted to particular machines.

A high level language program is translated into machine code by using either:

(i)   a compiler, which produces a machine code translation of a program, tests it for errors, stores the object program and executes it when instructed;

(ii)   an interpreter which executes the program as it translates it, thus producing no complete 'object program' at all.

(b) *Utility programs*

A utility is defined by the Chartered Institute of Management Accountants as:

'a program which performs a particular function that may be required by a number of other programs or in a number of circumstances...'

Certain tasks are common to all computer installations, for example:

- sorting of data into a sequence;
- copying files from one medium to another;
- reorganising files;
- transfer of data to a storage device;
- error detection.

Utility programs are made to avoid the need for separate programs to be developed to perform these tasks for each separate computer installation. They are thus sufficiently flexible to meet the requirement of most users.

(c) *Sub-routines*

Many programs require the same operation - eg a repeated calculation - to be performed at many points in the program.

Instead of writing out the detailed programming instructions each time the operation is required, the program can 'jump' to a sub-routine. A sub-routine will normally have a name, which will appear in the main program whenever the sub-routine is needed.

The sub-routine comprises the programming instructions for a particular operation. It need only be written once, and the program can refer to it any number of times.

The advantages of sub-routines are:

(i)   they save storage space;
(ii) programming time is reduced;
(iii) sub-routines can be developed separately from the main program;
(iv) fault-finding is easier in a program that has selected sub-routines;
(v)   they facilitate the creation of large programs, as sub-routines can be stored in 'libraries'.

(d) *Database management system*

A database contains data which can serve a number of different applications. The structure of the database is not determined by the structure of the applications.

Databases must be accessible directly and so are held on magnetic disk. Data is shared by a number of different users. The objective of a database is to minimise duplication of data between files. Data can be accessed and amended in a wide variety of ways.

A database management system (DBMS) is software that organises the database in the following ways.

(i) The DBMS builds database files. Certain requirements, such as the character length of each field, will have been specified by the user however.

(ii) The DBMS manages the database. The logical relationships between the items of data will have been determined by the programmer or systems analyst, but the physical storage is entirely independent of these logical relationships. The DBMS arranges the physical storage where particular items of data are located on disk, for example.

(iii) The DBMS provides the interface between application programs and the database itself. Any programs that require a specified output can only access the data through the DMBS.

(iv) The DBMS manages the updating and deletion of whatever files have been created in the database.

(e) *Data dictionary*

A data dictionary is part of the database management system.

(i) It details what categories of data are held. A category is sometimes be referred to as an 'entity' which is an item about which data is stored. An 'account', in an accounting database, is an 'entity'.

(ii) It describes what characteristics the data has. These are sometimes referred to as 'attributes'. For example, an 'account' will have an 'opening balance'. The 'opening balance' is an attribute of the entity 'account'.

(iii) It delineates the relationships between different entities.

(iv) It lists the data processing functions of the various entities described above.

Thus, a data dictionary provides a guide as to where an item of data is to be found in the logical structure of a database. This helps ensure that different programs work consistently. As it displays the relationships that types of data have with each other, the effects of amendments over the entire database can be easily foreseen. For a large database, a dictionary is essential to avoid corruption of the database.

41 BASIC REVISION QUESTION: PACKAGES

Application packages are ready-made programs written to perform a particular job. The job will be common to many potential users, so that the package could be adopted by all of them for their data processing operations. An application package may therefore be defined as 'a complete system for a particular application and supplied by some outside body for general use by individual firms. They use customer data to provide user departments with information and may be used by more than one installation or organisation'. The package must be fully documented and the documentation should include specifications of input and output formats and file layouts, user instruction manuals, hardware requirements and details of how the package may be varied to suit the user's individual needs.

General packages are, as their name suggests, more general in their application. The program can perform a specific function (eg spreadsheet modelling) but it is up to the customer whether it is used for stock, payroll etc.

An example of a general package is a spreadsheet package. There is simply a table with many columns and rows, used to insert tabulated data. Cash budgets and operating budgets are only two potential applications. One advantage is that amendments can be made very quickly and easily. Sensitivity analysis in budgeting, for example, becomes a simple matter of making small amendments to basic data, and obtaining revised figures.

42 OPERATING SYSTEMS

> *Tutorial note*. Part (a) of this question tests your knowledge of system software which users are likely to meet. A widespread operating system for microcomputers is MS-DOS. It was developed by the Microsoft Corporation and provides software services like those outlined below. (The question asks for *five* features.)

(a) The operating system (OS) is software which controls the resources within a data processing installation. It typically performs the following tasks.

   (1) Control of input/output data to and from the computer and peripheral devices. The OS will summon data from backing store, direct it to the CPU for processing, and sent it to output devices.

   (2) Management of *multitasking* (several programs competing for the processor's power at the same time) by allocation of priorities between different programs.

   (3) Calling up user application programs and system programs. Some of these may reside in backing store.

   (4) Allocation of random access memory. RAM memory contains data and programs currently executed. The OS will ensure that memory is used most efficiently.

   (5) Checking for errors in hardware, and handling unforeseen interruptions to program execution.

   (6) 'Booting' up the system (ie making it operational). The bootstrap program is normally held in ROM, and is usually activated when the computer is switched on.

   (7) Communication with users. The OS might send messages such as 'job complete'. The OS might received instructions in the form of a command language.

   (8) Store protection (keeping different programs separate in memory). This is very important in multitasking.

   Additionally, an operating system (eg MS-DOS) can be used to carry out a number of file handling tasks (eg copy, delete or rename a file; format a storage device such as a floppy disk).

(b) If a computer or a system is described as user-friendly, this implies that it has been designed to make it as simple as possible for users, who are not computer specialists or data processing professionals. User-friendly features include a 'help' facility, clear error messages, menus and so forth.

(c) A mouse is a small device which is connected by a cable to the basic module of a computer keyboard. The mouse is rolled on its hard ball over the desk top, and this movement is reflected in a corresponding motion of a pointer on the VDU screen.

The mouse is often used to direct a pointer to a menu, or an icon representing a task (eg a dustbin for file delete), and the option on the menu or indicated by the icon is selected and executed, by the depression of a button on the mouse. The *icon* is thus useful for representing data processing tastes in a colloquial way.

Mice, icons, and pointers are used because many computer users are not properly trained to use a keyboard, which is based on the traditional typewriter.

The generic term to this kind of interface is WIMP (window, icon, mouse, pulldown-menu).

A *menu* presents commands or options in a structured hierarchical way, guiding the user through the choices available.

A WIMP interface was an important development by Apple Computers.

43 WIMP OPERATING SYSTEM

> *Tutorial note.* When this question was set in the examination, candidates' main mistakes were in part (a) to write a full explanation of the role of the operating system and in part (b) to omit the requested diagram.

(a) The operating system is the bridge between the computer and the application programs and data. If you use a microcomputer with a hard disk, on which is stored a number of software programs (for example a spreadsheet, and a database and a word processing package) you will probably have to go out of the program you are using, into the operating system, which you will instruct to load up with the other systems under your remit. In some software packages (eg Lotus 123) there is a System command. You can temporarily hand control back to the OS to delete a file.

Data and programs are held in files on a storage medium, such as a hard disk. Sometimes you need to carry out various operations with these files as files (eg copy an entire file) which are a bit difficult or time consuming to carry out from within the application.

The operating system in many microcomputers provides a number of file maintenance commands and facilities. Strictly speaking, these are *utility programs*, but they are provided with many of the standard operating systems software currently available.

Some file commands available in MS-DOS are listed below.

COPY. Copy files, so that one version can be given a different name and then altered, or transferred copied on to another disk (eg for security, or to input elsewhere).
DEL. Delete a file.
DIR. List all the files in a particular directory.
DISKCOPY. This commands copies entire floppy disks.
ERASE. This is an alternative to DEL.
FIND. This searches files for a string of text.
FORMAT. This formats a disk, so it can be used as backing store.
MKDIR. A directory is a way of organising files on a disk. This commands is used to create a directory.
REN. This renames a file.
RESTORE. This restores backup diskette files to a hard disk.

(b) The use of a mouse, icons, and pulldown menus are part of a WIMP system (Windows, Icons, Mouse, Pulldown menu) which is a type of graphic user interface. Instead of typing in commands, the user selects icons with the mouse-controlled cursor.

The mouse is an object wired to the keyboard. It is a ball which is rolled along the top of the table, and its movement there corresponds to the movement of the cursor on screen. Once the required position of the cursor is reached, a switch on the mouse's top is depressed to execute the command

The cursor will be directed to options for menus. A menu bar at the top of a screen will indicate a number of options. Moving the cursor to the menu enables that menu to be pulled down, like a venetian blind, to the screen.

Alternatively, the cursor can be directed to an icon. An icon is a picture which represents a process. To delete a file might mean going to an icon of a dustbin. It is felt that icons are easier to remember than commands.

A picture of a screen is given below.

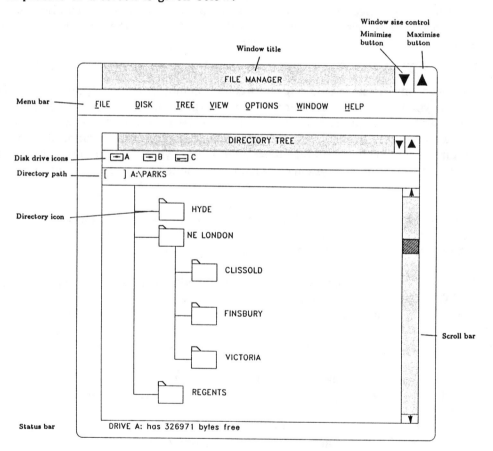

44 BASIC REVISION QUESTION: SPREADSHEETS

A spreadsheet is a type of software package often used for financial modelling. Input is via a VDU and keyboard. Output is displayed on a VDU and can often be printed. Structured like a piece of paper, a spreadsheet is split horizontally into 'rows' and vertically into 'columns'. Thus a spreadsheet is divided into 'cells'. Each cell has an 'address'. The cell where column A intersects with row 1 is referred to as cell A1.

Columns

		A	B	C	D
	1	Year	1989		
	2	Sales	100		
Rows	3	Costs	50		
	4	Gross profit	50		
	5 etc				

In a typical spreadsheet, the *contents* of a cell can be values, labels or automated commands.

A *value* can either be:

● a numeric amount that can be processed arithmetically with other numeric amounts;
● a formula, for example adding two cells together.

A *label* can be:

● a word;
● a number, such as a date, preceded by a 'label' marker, which makes it unusable in arithmetical operations.

An *automated command* is a type of label which acts as a program to carry out a number of separate operations in one key-stroke. This is sometimes referred to as a *macro*.

The cell will not necessarily *display* its contents. Cell B1 in the example may contain '1989, where the sign 'indicates that this is a label and not a value. It will only display 1989. It is the year, and forms part of the text, not part of the arithmetic.

The contents of cell B4 might be the formula +B2 - B3, subtracting the values in cell B3 from the values in cell B2. The cell *displays* the result of that calculation. This formula will be executed whatever the values in cells B2 and B3. Formulae may be of considerable complexity. Some spreadsheets provide functions to perform statistical calculations.

A spreadsheet may be up to 250 columns wide and 8,000 rows deep. As it is impossible therefore to see the entire spreadsheet at once, the user can scroll up, down or across the sheet. To move from one cell to another requires the use of a cursor. Data can only be entered on cells where the cursor resides, unless the user programs the spreadsheets otherwise.

A spreadsheet will contain additional features:

edit	-	to change the contents of a cell;
copy	-	copy a cell;
move	-	to move the contents of a cell to another cell;
range	-	to designate certain cells as a separate range;
format	-	to increase or decrease column widths, to present numbers in different ways (in financial format, for example, or to a specified number of decimal places);
print	-	so that the spreadsheet can be printed;
save	-	so that the contents of the spreadsheet can be saved as a *file* of data;
combine	-	function, to access data from other spreadsheet files;
translate	-	so that data held in one type of spreadsheet software can be transferred into another type of spreadsheet software.

45 SPREADSHEET FACILITIES

> *Tutorial note.* This is a practical question offering you an opportunity to score highly. Spreadsheets are something every computer user is likely to come across and so the examiner will expect you at the very least to be familiar with them and also, if you wish to do really well, to have had some practical experience of them.

A spreadsheet is a software program that provides the user with facilities for modelling and manipulating data, principally numerical data. A spreadsheet is a grid, structured like a sheet of paper divided into columns and rows. The intersection of a row and a column is called a cell. So, where row 1 intersects with column A the cell is known as cell A1.

A cell can contain text (eg Sales), numbers which can be used in arithmetical calculations, a formula, or a macro. Formulae are the key to a spreadsheet's model building prowess, and its use in what-if analysis. A formula normally refers to other cells, to perform some processing operation on them. For example, if cell C3 contains the formula A2*B1, then in cell C3 the results of multiplying the contents of cell A2 by cell B1 will be displayed. So, if the value in cell A2 is 10 and the value in cell B2 is 5, then cell C3 will display the value 50. Should cell A2 be changed to 20, then the display in cell C3 will automatically be altered to 100. While the cursor is on a particular cell, the contents of that cell are shown at the bottom of the screen. So while cell C3 would display 50 (or 100), the formula would also be shown at the bottom of the screen.

You are to set up a simple balance sheet, in such a way that you could use it to estimate how the balance sheet figures will change in total when any individual item in the balance sheet is altered.

Inserting text

The various headings required on the balance sheet are entered. This is done by means of a facility within the program which enables you to specify the text for any column, combined columns or rows of data. (It is usually convenient to start the tabulation at row 1 and column A, although this is not essential).

At this stage, your screen might look as follows.

	: A	:	B	: C	:
1:			**Current**	**year**	
2:			**£'000**	**£'000**	
3:	Fixed assets: gross value				
4:	accumulated depreciation				
5:	net book value				
6:	Current assets:				
7:	Stocks				
8:	Debtors				
9:	Cash				
10:					
11:	Current liabilities:				
12:	Overdraft				
13:	Creditors				
14:	Taxation				
15:					
16:	Net current assets				
17:					
18:	Total assets less current liabilities				

Inserting formulae

The next stage in constructing a model is to put in the calculations you want the computer to carry out, expressed as formulae.

Formulae required for this balance sheet are as follows.

- in cell B10   + B7 + B8 + B9 (or, alternatively, @ SUM(B7..B9)
- in cell B15;   + B12 + B13 + B14 (or, alternatively, @ SUM(B12..B14)
- in cell C5:   + C3 - C4
- in cell C16;   + B10 - B15
- in cell C18;   + C5 + C16, alternatively + C5 + B10 - B15

(Tutorial note. Although the example only uses plus and minus functions most spreadsheets are capable of using virtually any mathematical function, including multiplication of data in two or more cells, division, multiplication of items by a 'constant' factor, square roots and logical functions (eg IF B6 < 50 THEN C15 = 2,000). The functions can be combined to make exceedingly complicated formulae which would take a vary long time to compute by hand - remember, a formula can be up to about 100 characters long.)

Inserting data

The last stage in setting up a spreadsheet is to input data. In our example, suppose stocks are £5m, debtors £2,500,000 and cash £1,800,000. This 'raw data' would be input as figures into cells B7, B8 and B9 respectively, and the computer will automatically show the total in cell B10, using the formula already specified in the model. Other data would be input to cells C3, C4, B12, B13 and B14.

An extract from your completed balance sheet might look like this:

	A	B	C
	:	:	:
1:		Current	year
2:		£'000	£'000
3:	Fixed assets: gross value		17,000
4:	accumulated depreciation		6,750
5:	net book value		10,250
6:	Current assets:		
7:	stocks	5,000	
8:	debtors	2,500	
9:	cash	1,800	
10:		9,300	
11:	Current liabilities:		
12:	overdraft	600	
13:	creditors	1,200	
14:	taxation	800	
15:		2,600	
16:	Net current assets		6,700
17:			
18:	Total assets less current liabilities		16,950

If the contents of cell C3 (being £17,000 fixed assets) were altered to 18,000, the net book value displayed in cell C4 would change to 11,250 and the total assets less current liabilities displayed in cell C18 would change to 17,950.

46 BASIC REVISION QUESTION: WORD PROCESSOR

There are many factors to be considered when selecting a computer package, whether it is a word processing package or some other application under scrutiny. Some of the more important questions to ask if a department is thinking about buying a word processor are:

(a) does the department need only a dedicated word processor, or would it also be able to make use of the facilities offered by a mini-computer or microcomputer?

(b) how many keyboards and VDUs are likely to be needed?

(c) is the word processor easy to use? Is the explanatory documentation clear? Are courses available to train operators, if training is needed?

(d) is the word processor able to use the software best suited to the department?

(e) what quality (and speed) of printed output is available?

(f) what back-up facilities are available in the event of a breakdown? Is the supplying company stable? (ie is it going to be around to help out in the event of a failure?);

(g) is the word processor compatible with other computer configurations within the department, if any?

47 WORD PROCESSING AND DESK-TOP PUBLISHING

Tutorial note. The examiner commented that he was surprised at the poor quality of answers on word processing and that few candidates had any real understanding of desk-top publishing. This emphasises how important it is to keep up with the more recent developments in hardware and software.

(a) Word processing is the use of a computer and related technology to create, manipulate, edit and print text and text files. Word processing applications are commonly purchased as packages for a microcomputer, although in the past many word processing systems were stand-alone on dedicated terminals. A typical word processing application will feature the following.

(1) File creation, and file handling. A document is created, saved, and retrieved for further use, as a computer file.

(2) Text editing. A number of features are supported here. Blocks of text can be moved around the document. Typing mistakes can be overwritten, and amended. Text can be inserted into, or deleted from, other pieces of text.

(3) Document design. Word processing packages enable tabulations, justification, margins and page heading and so forth to be set. It is possible to ensure that some words are printed in bold or italics, in short that different fonts can be used (all this requires a laser printer). Some advanced packages offer a *style sheet* to the user: a particular font, and type size can be assigned a name and stored for later use to format a whole document or portion thereof.

(4) Merging. Text from two or more documents (ie separate computer text files) can be combined in one document.

(5) Spelling checker. Most word processing packages offer a lexicon of commonly used words. These are compared to input text and any words found in the document which are not contained in the lexicon are brought to the attention of the user for amendment or for addition to the lexicon.

(6) Calculator. Many word processing packages contain a simple calculator facility. This is quite useful for financial information.

(7) Import data from other applications. A feature of more recent word processing applications is one which enables a graphic image to be placed within a text document. Also, some can import data from a spreadsheet application into a table, usually a fixed format.

(8) Macros. Many word processing packages offer a facility to automate frequently repeated sequences of key strokes so that they can be executed in one operation.

(9) Mailmerge. A standard letter can be written, and a list of names and addresses can be input to the computer, to be inserted into the standard format.

(10) Some word processing packages (eg Wordperfect 5.1) can be used on a number of operating systems.

(b) Desk-top publishing is a term used to describe the production of attractive documents for publication using a computer system. As such, it might seem like word processing, but desk top publishing does not deal so much with the mechanics of text editing and creation. Rather, desk-top publishing applications computerise the formatting, typesetting, and layout of documents. Some word processing packages offer such features, but they are generally not as flexible as those offered by a desk-top publishing application.

A number of features merit some attention.

(1) WYSIWYG (What you see is what you get) will always be offered by a DTP package. The user is able to see exactly how a page will appear in print.

(2) Output needs to be sent to a normal text printer (eg a laser) for text correction, or an image setter or typesetter for final copy.

(3) Graphics import. DTP enables pictures and diagrams to be imported from an external source, and then enlarged, reduced and cut as required. Some DTP packages (eg 3B2) enable some graphics to be drawn from scratch. A scanner might be used to import these pictures.

It may not seem that an accounts department would have much use for a very sophisticated DTP package. However, providing it was easy to use, a DTP package would be invaluable in producing documents of a financial nature that are easy read.

48   DATA MANAGEMENT SOFTWARE

(a) A data management software package provides users with the facility to construct and use a simple database, with a limited number of fields and records. It is normally comprised of a single file. This is called a flat file database.

The user sets up the required database structure. The package enables data to be easily manipulated, sorted, edited and merged as appropriate, and in fact the whole database can be restructured without any loss of data.

The package may include a facility that permits the design of menus. A menu offers a number of choices of action in a structured way. The menus can therefore be designed to offer a choice between a number of programs. Alternatively, a menu can request information about the type of data to be accessed.

The package may permit the actual formats of output to be designed on the screen. Alternatively, it can allow the user to define the reports desired, by selecting a number of different data items.

Input, too, may be made more user-friendly by providing a strict format on-screen. This reduces the likelihood of input errors. An editing facility, allowing data to be 'confirmed' before it is entered, may be provided. The data as entered will appear on the screen, but a separate keystroke will be needed to use it to update the files.

(b) One example can be seen in an organisation that sells its products by 'direct mail' ('junk mail').

It could build up a database containing information about its customers, and so it could 'target' its mail more effectively to those customers likely to respond.

Such data would include:

(i)   the customer's name;
(ii)   address;
(iii) a brief note as to whether the customer has responded to direct mail before;
(iv)   other personal details about the customer, for example age, sex, marital status, occupation etc.

This data can be used in a number of ways. For example, the company could decide to send letters only to accounting technicians over 25 years old living in Basildon.

(c)   The disadvantages of these systems are:

(i)   they do not allow for a great deal of sophistication, as they are designed for simplicity;
(ii)   that, sometimes, a tailor-made software package for a particular application may be more appropriate to the company's needs;
(iii) many users may spend time inventing reports which are broadly similar in content, thus duplicating effort.

49 DATABASE MANAGEMENT

> *Tutorial note.* The examiner commented that many candidates did not read this question carefully when attempting it in the examination. In part (a) many answers related to the process of building up a file and to the file itself rather than to the *features* of the package. In part (b), candidates ignored the request for two *menu* screens and gave detailed output screens instead.

(a)   A database management system allows the user to build and manage a database and provides the user with access to that database. There are four main steps in the operation of a DBMS.

(i)   creation of database structure
(ii)   entry/amendment of data
(iii) retrieval and manipulation of data
(iv)   report production.

(i)   The user specifies what file or files are to be held in the database, sets out the records and fields to be held in each and specifies the maximum number of characters per field. Each should be named, eg customer name, telephone number, address, customer contact, in-house contact etc. Characteristics of each field are specified (eg all numeric, all alphabetical, alpha-numeric) and the record should be laid out on screen in a format which is easy to use and to update.

(ii)   Once the database structure has been established and the screen formats defined, the user can input data to create a file. Because it is vital that databases are kept up to date, a number of commands may be required. As an example of this, the dBase III plus package offers the following 'update' sub-menu:

Append
Edit Display
Browse Replace
Delete Recall Pack

The commands to note here are Append, Edit, Browse and Delete (the others being variations on those four).

(iii) The database is now ready for use. Data can be retrieved by specifying the required parameters, eg customers who have been on the database for over two years but who have not placed an order in that period, or customers who are based in Scotland who have responded to a particular mailshot. Data retrieved in this way can then be sorted according to any specified field, eg business done in the last year, size of company, geographical location.

(iv) Reporting can be done, either on screen or to hard copy. Report formats can be defined and stored so that they do not need to be redesigned each time the user requests a report.

(b) (i)

CUSTOMER CONTACTS SYSTEM	
UPDATE MENU	
Add new record	1
Amend data	2
Delete record	3
Enquiry	4
Print record	5
Return to main menu	6

(ii)

CUSTOMER CONTACTS SYSTEM	
RETRIEVAL MENU	
Build search condition	1
Build scope condition	2
Display on screen	3
Display on printer	4
Return to main menu	5

50 SOFTWARE APPLICATIONS

Tutorial note. This question shows that it is not enough to know about spreadsheets, word-processors and databases alone. You would be penalised in an exam if you failed to indicate a possible use of each package.

(a) *Desk-top publishing* is a development from word processing which allows sophisticated manipulation of documents, notably in the areas of typesetting and composition. Word processing is ideal for letters and reports which consist purely of text, but when it is desired to include diagrams, photographs, graphs and tables in a report, the average WP package does not offer the facilities to enable this to be achieved easily. DTP systems present the page on screen in the form in which it will be published (WYSIWYG; what you see is what you get, is necessary for this), and allow the user to move blocks of the page around. Text and graphics are usually imported from other systems and can be set together on a page. Graphics can be enlarged or reduced to best effect. DTP systems require a high quality printer, usually a laser printer, and operate well with a mouse, as this facilitates marking points on a page.

A typical application of DTP would be in the preparation of an in-house magazine.

(b) *Financial modelling* usually involves the performance of some kind of sensitivity analysis or 'what if?' analysis on a set of financial data. A user might wish to examine the effect of increases in material costs on a projected profit and loss account or the effect of delays in payments to creditors on a projected cashflow forecast. There are a number of specialised modelling packages available, but many users utilise a spreadsheet for this kind of exercise. Variables can be changed or formulae adjusted and the model recalculated to review the effect of the new assumption.

A company treasurer would be likely to use a financial modelling package.

(c) *Expert systems* are computer programs which allow users to benefit from expert knowledge and information, and also advice. An expert system is a program for which the knowledge base file holds a large amount of specialised data, eg on legal, engineering or medical information, or tax matters. The user keys in certain facts and the program uses its information on file to produce a decision about something on which an expert's decision would normally be required. For example a user without a legal background can obtain guidance on the law without having to consult a solicitor, for example on property purchase matters, or for company law guidance.

Banks may use expert systems for the purpose of assessing the creditworthiness of a bank customer applying for a loan.

(d) *Presentation graphics* are programs which allow the user to build up a series of graphical displays or images for use in a presentation. The graphics can be transferred to 35mm slides, overhead projector slides or on to a computer screen projection. The software offers a range of icons, maps, shapes and symbols which can be coloured or 'rearranged' as required. Text can be incorporated and manipulated in a similar way to WP text.

Presentation graphics might be used at a sales conference.

51 BUSINESS SYSTEMS

> *Tutorial note.* A variety of alternatives could have been offered in part (a) from word processing to more advanced just-in-time applications. You were only required to describe *two* systems, other than accounting or payroll applications. You were required to list only *ten* questions to ask a supplier in part (b).

(a) *Business systems*

Word processing

A company which has no computer experience obviously has no experience of word processing, which is the manipulation of textual, and occasional graphical data on screen and in the memory of a computer. This would be used in the organisation's:

- internal correspondence (memoranda);
- external correspondence (letters);
- marketing the products (mail shots could be expedited by mail merge);
- management information systems (eg to type the monthly management accounts).

Database

A small database system could be used to keep product and customer information. So, it would be possible, for example, to use the database to provide management reports as to which products sold well, or which type of customer bought which product. There might be regional variations in selling patterns, which could be highlighted by a database. A database might enable the company to analyse some of its information in more detail.

Computer-aided design

Small companies can produce advanced and sophisticated products, but research and development can be expensive. CAD software might make R & D cheaper, as various designs could be tried out on the computer and analysed for their effectiveness. It also reduces the time taken to produce technical drawings.

Stock control system

The aim of a such a system would be to keep a record of each item of stock, stating how much of it is available, at a particular time. Such a system could be used:

- to monitor stock levels, generating orders for stock automatically;
- as an aid in production planning, as if the company has to wait for an item of stock to be delivered, then production will be hard to plan properly;
- valuation for year end accounts purposes.

Materials resource planning

These are techniques which control the input of materials and subcomponents into a production system. A materials resource planning system is one by which the production is planned backwards, as it were, from the finished goods output required to components and sub-assemblies and back to raw materials requirements. Production times and lead times are built into the system, so that the exact requirements at any particular time for raw materials can be estimated.

Just-in-time systems

Just-in-time systems are a type of stock control system, but which seek to minimise the holding of stocks of raw materials or finished goods as it is felt that the cost of holding them is greater than people have estimated previously.

Order processing

This is particularly appropriate if the company makes bespoke products to order, or, indeed, if flexible manufacturing systems are employed. An order processing system will enable the status of each order at any stage in the production process to be accessed easily, enabling rescheduling of late orders, completion time estimates and so forth to be made accurately.

(b)   The following information would be asked of a supplier of a software package.

    (i)   How well established is the supplier?

    (ii)   Is the package *compatible* with the company's existing hardware.

    (iii)   Does the package require more powerful hardware than what is currently possessed?

    (iv)   Can the package be integrated with the company's current software, if this is desired (eg as input to a management information system).

    (v)   Does the package have user-friendly features (eg a graphic user interface)?

    (vi)   Has the package been widely adopted? If not, is it possible to meet other users of the package, to learn from their experience.

    (vii)   Is the package properly documented?

    (viii)   Will the supplier or software house provide training?

    (ix)   Will the supplier or software house provide a help line, so that problems can be ironed out quickly?

    (x)   How much does the package cost?

    (xi)   How costly will be any alterations to adapt the package to the environment in which it will be operating?

    (xii)   Will there be any upgrades offered, and if so, will these be offered at favourable rates?

    (xiii)   Is there an adequate warranty offered, so that the company can be compensated if the package does not perform to the agreed specification.

    (xiv)   Does the supplier offer any financing arrangement that might be useful?

52 INTEGRATED SYSTEMS: NOMINAL LEDGER

Integrated systems can be defined as 'a number of systems which, although capable of autonomous operation, may be linked closely to form a comprehensive single view to the user' (CIMA). The use of common files by the individual systems is a feature of integration.

(a)   In an integrated sales, purchase and nominal ledger system transactions in the sales and purchase ledgers will be automatically reflected in the nominal ledger. Transactions need only be input once. In a non-integrated system, with completely separate files, identical items of data have to be input more often. Cash received from a debtor, for example, would have to be input first to the customer's account in the sales ledger application, and second to the sales ledger control and cash accounts in the nominal ledger application.

In an integrated system:

(i)   output from one 'system' can be used as input for another;
(ii)   master files can be combined;
(iii) data is input once, minimising clerical effort and ensuring all applications process the same data.

(b)   A nominal ledger system is simply a computer system that performs the essential double entry bookkeeping to produce a trial balance at the end of a particular accounting period. This is then used to prepare a set of accounts.

A nominal ledger system may have any number of the features outlined below.

(i)   A coding system for:
●   accounts;
●   cost centres;
●   departments and subdivisions
●   other group companies (if there are several).

A good nominal ledger system will also permit the addition and deletion of codes no longer used.

(ii)   A journal facility for period-end adjustments; accruals are made at the end of an accounting period, and are revoked at the beginning of a new period.

(iii) Comparisons with prior periods, and/or with budget.

(iv)   A multiple currency facility (in a large organisation which uses more than one currency, or which trades internationally).

(v)   Automatic calculation of VAT on certain transactions.

(vi)   Facilities for consolidating departments, or subsidiary companies.

A nominal ledger system that is integrated with the sales ledger system may work in a variety of ways. For example, when cash is received from a debtor, the double entry is:

Dr   Cash   Cr Debtors

In a non-integrated system, postings are made, in the nominal ledger, to the cash account and to the sales ledger account. In addition, the sales ledger, containing details of each customer's balance, must be updated. The sales ledger is, in effect, memorandum information.

In an integrated system, updating the sales ledger also updates the nominal ledger at the same time. The sales ledger is not simply memorandum information and forms part of the double entry.

A system integrating the nominal ledger with the sales ledger, for example, may operate by batch processing. Individual movements on debtor accounts in the sales ledger, (cash receipts, sales etc) are aggregated over the month, and in a single month-end run, both the nominal ledger and the sales ledger are updated.

Alternatively in a real-time system, the postings will be made as and when the transaction occurs.

53 DECISION TABLE

Tutorial note. The method you should use to construct a decision table is to:

(a) list the conditions;
(b) list the actions;
(c) calculate the number of rules and draw the necessary columns;
(d) apply the halving rule to enter the 'Y's and 'N's (standing for 'yes' and 'no');
(e) work down the resulting rules, and enter X for the appropriate actions.

For the stock system in question, the *conditions* are:

(a) Is there sufficient stock to cover the order?
(b) Is stock level zero?
(c) Has adjusted balance fallen below re-order level?
(d) Is an order outstanding?

The *actions* are:

(a) adjust stock balance, send papers to despatch;
(b) complete an order form;
(c) photocopy order form;
(d) put order form into outstanding requisitions file;
(e) send urge note to factory;
(f) telephone factory.

There are four conditions, so there ought to be $2^4 = 16$ columns in the decision table. Some of the combinations will prove to be impossible, others will be duplicated: nevertheless, the best way to proceed is to draw out the full table and then prune it to a smaller one.

Rule	1	2	3	4	5	6	7	8	9	10	11	12	13	14	15	16
Conditions																
Sufficient stock to cover order?	Y	Y	Y	Y	Y	Y	Y	Y	N	N	N	N	N	N	N	N
Stock level zero?	Y	Y	Y	Y	N	N	N	N	Y	Y	Y	Y	N	N	N	N
Adjusted balance below re-order level?	Y	Y	N	N	Y	Y	N	N	Y	Y	N	N	Y	Y	N	N
Order outstanding?	Y	N	Y	N	Y	N	Y	N	Y	N	Y	N	Y	N	Y	N
Actions	Impossible															
Adjust balance: papers to be despatched					X	X	X	X					X	X	X	X
Complete order form						X				X		X		X		X
Put into o/s reqs. file									X	X	X	X	X	X	X	X
Photocopy order form													X	X	X	X
Send urge note to factory									X		X		X		X	
Telephone factory									X		X					

(It is assumed that even if the factory has made an order, details will still be input to the requisition file).

The last step is to simplify this decision table, by noticing that:

(a) if there is sufficient stock to cover an order, then clearly the stock level cannot be zero; therefore four of the columns are impossible;

(b) in several instances, the actions to be taken are identical, so the relevant conditions can be merged;

The resulting decision table looks like this:

Rule	(5)	(6)	(7&8)	(9&11)	(10&12)	(13&15)	(14&16)
Conditions							
Sufficient stock to cover order?	Y	Y	Y	N	N	N	N
Stock level zero?				Y	Y	N	N
Adjusted balance below re-order level?	Y	Y	N				
Order outstanding	Y	N		Y	N	Y	N
Actions							
Adjust balance: papers to despatch	X	X	X			X	X
Complete order form		X			X		X
Put into o/s requisitions file				X	X	X	X
Photocopy form						X	X
Send urge note to factory	X			X		X	
Telephone factory					X		

54 FLOWCHART

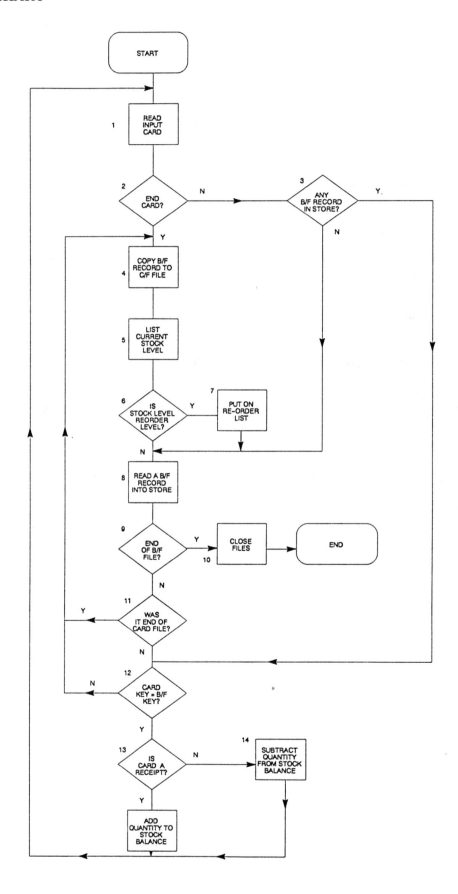

55 LOGICAL REPRESENTATION

> *Tutorial note.* This was a popular question when it appeared in the examination. Part (a) was very well done. Part (b) was usually tackled by means of a decision table, although some candidates chose to use other approaches including tree diagrams and BASIC programs. These were equally valid.

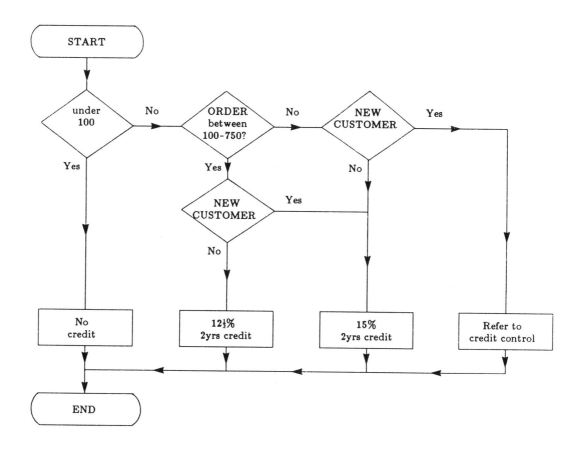

DECISION TABLE

Under 100	Y	N	N	N	N
£100 – £750	N	N	Y	N	N
Over £750	N	Y	N	Y	N
New customer	N/A	Y	N	Y	N
No credit	✓				
2 years at 12½%			✓		
2 years at 15%		✓			✓
Credit control				✓	

56 BASIC REVISION QUESTION: LANGUAGES

(a) A high level language is a language used by programmers to tell a computer what to do, regardless of which low level (machine) language the computer uses. Program-writing time is much reduced because a single high level language instruction can generate many low level language instructions - so programs written in a high level language are shorter than those written in a low level language.

High level language is relatively easy to learn, and once a program is written in a high-level language, it need not be revised again and again to suit the language needs of different computers; it just needs to be compiled into the relevant low level (machine) language.

(b) (i)   FORTRAN stands for Formula Translation and is a scientific language designed primarily for the easy expression of mathematical formulae.

(ii)   ALGOL stands for Algorithmic Language, and is an algebraic language used for scientific purposes.

(iii) PL/1 stands for Programming Language One. It was developed to combine both scientific and commercial facilities.

(iv)   COBOL stands for Common Business Oriented Language, and is the most commonly used commercial language. Designed by an international committee known as CODASYL (Cobol is referred to as a codasyl language), it uses English style statements and is suitable for batch processing programming and, in the latest variations (eg ANSI Cobol) for interactive programming.

(v)   BASIC stands for Beginners All Purpose Symbolic Instruction Code. It is an easy language to learn and is widely used in educational establishments in time sharing applications and for home computers.

57 BASIC REVISION QUESTION: STRUCTURED TECHNIQUES

Programming by structured techniques is called *structured programming*.

With structured programming, the overall problem is sub-divided into parts, which are then sub-divided further and further until the small sub-divisions consist of logic which can be converted fairly readily into program code. Block diagrams are used to structure the problem into these sub-divisions or *modules*, which then provide the basis for program preparation and coding, without the need to construct flowcharts.

One way of describing this form of structured programming is as *top-down programming* (breaking large and complex tasks into successively smaller sections).

58 TERMINOLOGY IN PROGRAMMING

> *Tutorial note.* In terminology questions like this, it is always going to be extremely difficult to obtain 5 marks if you do not produce five points on each matter. Try to produce a definition and description of the term, describe an application, list its main features and set out its advantages and disadvantages. These categories may not always be appropriate, but should give you a start.

(a) *High level language*

A computer is basically a collection of tiny electronic circuits that can be switched ON or OFF. Some of these circuits form the memory of the computer, some the arithmetic and logic unit to carry out the processing, and some the control unit. Anything the computer does therefore is ultimately reduceable to the switching ON and OFF of electric circuits in a particular sequence.

These two states can be represented by the binary digits 1 and 0. To instruct the computer to do anything, the instructions are written in this binary form, basically saying which circuits are switched ON and which are switched OFF.

Writing computer code in this simple binary form is terribly time consuming, and difficult, as everything the computer does has to be mapped out in detail. Computer programs written in this binary form are said to be in machine code.

Assembly languages, which abbreviated instructions, were developed to speed up the task, but they still required programmers to mimic the way a machine carried out the task, rather than write a program according to its own process logic.

High level languages, such as BASIC, COBOL, PASCAL, C were developed to make programming even quicker. The programs written in these languages, whilst highly formal, followed the logic of the process rather than its physical implementation on the computer. Unlike machine code, or assembly languages high level languages are not machine specific. It is possible, for example, to write a BASIC program which will work on many makes of computer. A program written in assembly language or machine code is not transportable in this way.

High level languages are translated into machine code by a compiler or interpreter program.

(b) *Object program*

Most programs are written in high level languages (see (a) above). However, a program written in COBOL or BASIC cannot be immediately run on the computer because, as we have seen, a computer can only handle instructions in binary form, that is, in machine code.

Compiler programs or interpreter programs are used to translate a program written in a high level language into machine code. A program written in an assembly language also has to be translated into machine code, and this is done by an assembly program.

It is common to refer to the program written in the high level (or assembly) language as the source program. The object program is the machine code version of this program after it has been translated.

Note that a compiler translates the program before the processing begins, but that interpreter program (often used with BASIC) translates it line by line.

(c) *Logic error*

A program is a sequence of instructions, a bit like a recipe. However, a program can contain flaws. Syntax errors are those flaws which result from an incorrect use of the programming language. For example, if, in a hypothetical language every word has to be followed by a line {LIKE_THIS} and this rule is not obeyed {LIKE THIS} then the program would fail.

A logic error on the other hand has little to do with the programming language, but is instead an error or inconsistency in the program. A logic error in a program is one whereby the program failed because it has been asked to do something logically impossible, or for some other reason it cannot proceed. For example, if the program was to repeat an instruction, and the number of times the instruction was to be repeated was not given, then the computer would continue the instruction indefinitely. Another meaning of logic error is that a program functions properly but does something it was not supposed to do for example if a subtraction instruction had been replaced by an addition instruction.

(d) *Utility program*

There are certain types of jobs which are performed by every computer. It is obvious that if programs for these tasks were written separately for each installation there will be an enormous waste of programmers' time. The manufacturers and software houses, recognising this problem, have produced a wide range of programs designed to perform these routine jobs, with sufficient inbuilt flexibility to handle all users' requirements. A utility program is a 'systems program designed to perform a *commonplace task* such as the transfer of data from one storage device to another or sorting a set of data'.

Utility software is usually provided by the computer manufacturer with the computer, perhaps as resident software in the computer's memory. Utility programs are often available with the operating system.

The main types of *utility software* available are as follows.

(i) *File conversion* - transferring file data from one medium to another (eg punched cards to magnetic tape; magnetic tape to line printer output).

(ii) *File copying (file dumping)* - copying files from one storage device to another (eg to copy data from a disk file on to another disk or tape streamer to produce a back-up copy of the file).

(iii) *Memory dumping* - copying the contents of the main store on to an output device (eg magnetic tape; line printer). A checkpoint/restart program dumps main store contents at periodic intervals and if something should go wrong, the application program can be restarted at the last checkpoint.

(iv) *File reorganisation* - when a disk file becomes too unwieldy to use, for instance if the overflow areas are almost full, it has to be reorganised. Utility software is provided to do this.

(v) *File maintenance (file modification)* - enables the user to create, delete and rename records; amend standing data etc.

(vi) A *diagnostic routine* or *debugging routine* provides for outline program testing and error correction during program development. When a programmer is testing a program, and the program does not operate correctly, he must locate the cause of the error. Diagnostic routines enable him to find out what the program was doing at the time it failed, and what the contents of store were etc.

(vii) *Sorting/merging* - enables records to be re-organised into the desired key-field sequence. The parameters of a sort program, which must be supplied for each application, are the key-field size and position, and the number and size of records. The computer programmer simply has to add the parameters for sorting (eg sorting by customer account code number) and can then use the utility sort program to provide the required sort program or sub-routine.

59 DP DEPARTMENT

Tutorial note. This question tests your knowledge of the structure of the data processing department and the activities of the various personnel involved. Note that the system is 'on-line', and therefore the managerial and operational roles are distinct from what you would find in a batch processing system.

(a) (A) Data processing manager;
(B) Operations manager;
(C) Systems analysts;
(D) Programmers;
(E) Computer operators.

(b) (A) *Data processing manager*

The data processing/computer manager is responsible for the efficient running of the department and must therefore be a good administrator as well as having some knowledge of data processing. His main duties are:

(i) planning and controlling the department;
(ii) supervising staff selection and training;
(iii) preparing budgets and ensuring they are adhered to;
(iv) liaising between general management and the technical members of his staff;
(v) reporting to senior management/board of directors/management services director on systems development and operations;
(vi) developing the DP systems, and ensuring they meet the needs of the business.

(B) *Operations manager*

As the system is on-line, the operations manager is not responsible for the preparation and input of data into the system. There is no need to schedule 'batch processing runs' as data is input at source and files are updated immediately.

The operations manager should, however:

(i) monitor the functioning of the equipment;
(ii) ensure there are no impediments to communications;
(iii) acquire the necessary materials and equipment so that the department functions smoothly;

(iv)   deal speedily with any problems (eg breakdowns), perhaps using the services of a team of specialist staff, or by contracting with the manufacturer's designers of the system;

(v)   ensure that file back-up procedures are carried out routinely (to retrieve data in case of breakdown);

(vi)   keep the DP manager informed of any important operational developments.

(E)   *Computer operators*

In a batch processing system computer operators 'run' the computer, loading input devices and files and initiating output runs.

However, in an 'on-line' environment, there is much less work to be done of a manual nature, and thus there will be fewer computer operators. Instead, an operator will be more of a 'technician' ensuring at detailed level that the system runs efficiently.

60 STAFF ROLES

Tutorial note. While it is true that a systems analyst analyses a system and a data preparation supervisor supervises the preparation of data, such explanations are rather too brief. The examiner expects rather more insight than this. The answers to parts (a), (b) and (e) below are longer than you would hope to achieve under exam conditions, but should be useful for revision purposes.

(a)   *Systems analyst*

In general terms, the tasks of the systems analyst are:

(i)   *systems analysis* - carrying out a methodical study of a current system (ie some data processing applications) to establish:

    (1)   what the current system does;

    (2)   what it ought to be able to achieve (ie whether it does what it is supposed to);

    (3)   what the user department would like the data processing system to do, and so what the required objectives of the system are.

The analysis of the current system might involve a manual data processing system or a system that is already computerised but could possibly be improved or modernised;

(ii)   *systems design* - having established what the proposed system objectives are, the next stage is to design a system that will achieve these requirements;

(iii)   *systems specification* - in designing a new system, it is the task of the systems analyst to specify the system in detail - its input, files, processing, output, hardware, costs, accuracy, response times etc. The system design is spelled out formally in a document or manual called the systems specification (which includes a program specification for each program in the system);

The systems specification has three uses:

- as a reference document for the systems analysts;
- as a document which can be studied by the management of the user department to check that the systems analysts are designing a system that will do what they want it to;
- as a document that computer programmers can use as the starting point for writing a program. Within the system specification, there will be a detailed specification for each program in the system.

(iv) *systems testing;*

(v) *keeping the system under review* - ie system maintenance.

(b) *File librarian*

The file librarian looks after the program files and data files. These are the physical tapes and disks used in the computer room. Obviously, files must not get mixed up, and it is essential to know which files contain what data, ie:

(i) which files contain the programs. What programs are held on each particular file;

(ii) which files contain certain master file or reference file data, and what files contain transactions data;

(iii) what 'generation' of data is held on a particular file. For example, there might be 3 files for a stock master file, covering 3 generations of data on the 'grandfather-father-son' principle described in an earlier chapter;

(iv) what files are blank or contain data that is not longer needed and so can be overwritten (purged). These files can be used as output files for future processing work;

(v) what files are 'back-up' files. For data security reasons, it is common to duplicate data on a file by copying it on to another 'back-up' file. If anything goes wrong with the original file, the back-up can be used in its place.

The librarian has the responsibility for keeping the file library, and so keeping a record of the data held on each file. He must also ensure that the data is kept physically secure (eg by locking the door to the file library when he is not in it). Finally, he has the task of sending the files to the computer room when they are needed, and receiving them back again when processing is finished. The data control clerks will tell the librarian what to send, and what data will be contained on the files that come back.

(c) *Data preparation supervisor*

Data preparation staff convert input data from a user department into a machine-sensible form, and so they are only required for batch processing work in systems where large volumes of data are input in batches, and are encoded on to disk or tape, or punched on to punch cards or paper tape, before input. Data preparation would involve encoding and verifying the data in time for the scheduled processing run of the computer.

The data preparation supervisor is responsible for organising this work - ie:

(i)   allocating batches of input to individual operators for encoding or punching;

(ii)   allocating encoded batches to other individual operators for verifying;

(iii) supervising the speed and quality of the work of individual operators;

(iv) carrying out normal supervisory duties - ie dealing with welfare problems and discipline problems etc;

(v)   ensuring that data preparation work is done on time;

(vi) ensuring that the staff can cope with the work load, otherwise making requests to the operations manager for more staff or more equipment.

(d)   *Computer maintenance engineer*

The role of the computer maintenance engineer is relatively simple to describe, and the duties are outlined in the job title. The computer maintenance engineer is employed, perhaps by the supplier, to provide hardware support to users. This can take a variety of forms: removing hardware for repair, repairing hardware on-site, and if necessary sorting out problems caused by errors in comprehension. The engineer may also be required to install hardware equipment.

(e)   *Data control clerk*

Data control clerks are responsible for receipt and despatch, and for getting processing 'jobs' ready for being carried out in the computer room. Receipt and despatch covers the physical receipt of data from the user department and the despatch of output (and the return of data documents).

A second aspect of data control work is to tell the computer operators what processing work to do.

(i)   Instructions about processing will be received from the user department or there will be a standing instruction about when processing will be done.

(ii)   Data control staff must ensure that input data will be available for the processing, and so control over receipt is necessary.

(iii) The data files for the processing must be specified and got ready. The data control clerk must therefore produce a list of what files will be needed, and ask the file librarian to send them to the computer room.

(iv) The data control clerk will specify the programs and files that must be used, and the input and output devices needed. These specifications will be sent to the computer room.

(v)   The data control clerk will also prepare the Job Control Language instructions to feed into the computer for the processing. The JCL commands will be acted on by the operating system in the CPU. (Note: a JCL is defined as a set of high-level instructions designed to enable a particular computer processing job or application to occur automatically without the need for operator intervention. The JCL commands are acted on by the operating system of the computer).

61   DATA PROCESSING STAFF

Tutorial note. The key to this question is successful identification of the word 'operations' in the question wording. If in doubt, have a look at the organisation chart, which shows clearly where the operations section is. The examiner gave credit for organisation charts where these were produced in the exam.

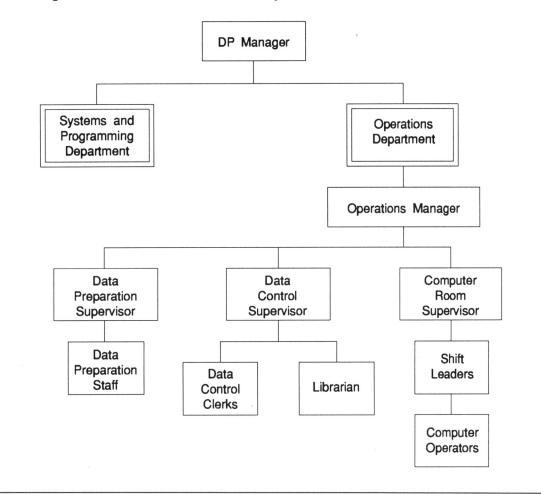

(a)   *Operations manager*

The operations manager is in charge of the activities of the data preparation section, the computer room and other sections in the computer centre. Operations staff in a DP department are the staff in the computer centre, and so obviously, they are only employed by an organisation with a mainframe computer or several mainframe computers in an operations centre.

The tasks of the operations manager are:

(i)   to provide a computer operations service to user departments, so that:

   (1)   data submitted for processing by a user department is properly prepared for input;
   (2)   prepared data is input for processing;
   (3)   output is sent to the user department, and input documents are also returned;
   (4)   data files are properly kept in a secure place.

In other words, the operations manager is responsible for the quality of these services;

(ii) to plan operations work ensuring that the computer centre has enough resources to meet the demand for data processing;

(iii) to arrange for adequate maintenance of the hardware;

(iv) to provide adequate security in the computer centre;

(v) to answer complaints about errors in processing that appear to be errors by operating staff (eg lost batches of input data, corrupted files and output, lost data files etc);

(vi) to ensure that procedures for operations work are properly implemented.

(b) *Data preparation supervisor*

Data preparation staff convert input data from a user department into a machine-sensible form, and so they are only required for batch processing work in systems where large volumes of data are input in batches, and are encoded on to disk or tape, or punched on to punch cards or paper tape, before input. Data preparation would involve encoding and verifying the data in time for the scheduled processing run of the computer.

The data preparation supervisor is responsible for organising this work - ie:

(i) allocating batches of input to individual operators for encoding or punching;
(ii) allocating encoded batches to other individual operators for verifying;
(iii) supervising the speed and quality of the work of individual operators;
(iv) carrying out normal supervisory duties - ie dealing with welfare problems and discipline problems etc;
(v) ensuring that data preparation work is done on time;
(vi) ensuring that the staff can cope with the work load, otherwise making requests to the operations manager for more staff or more equipment.

(c) *Data control supervisor*

Data control is concerned with the control of input data from the time it is received from a user department to the time it is returned:

(i) ensuring that output information is properly despatched;

(ii) ensuring that the appropriate data files are made available for processing when required, and that they are safely stored away from processing, if they are still needed for future use;

(iii) ensuring that the appropriate program files are made available for input to the CPU when required;

(iv) notifying the user department of any problems in processing, eg machine breakdowns that delay processing, or a high level of exception reports indicating serious errors in the input data;

(v)   informing the computer operators of the processing work to be done, so that the operators can carry out specific instructions (ie what program must be loaded into the computer, what Job Control Language instructions must be given to the computer's operating system, what data files should be loaded, what input data should be loaded, what output devices will be needed etc).

The data control supervisor has the overall responsibility for ensuring that this work is done properly. His staff consist of data control clerks and the file librarian.

(d) *Data control clerks*

The data control clerks are responsible for receipt and despatch, and for getting processing jobs ready to be carried out in the computer room. Receipt and despatch covers the physical receipt of data from the user department and the despatch of output (and return of 'source' data documents).

(e) *The file librarian*

The file librarian looks after the program files and data files. These are the physical tapes and disks used in the computer room. Obviously, files must not get mixed up, and it is essential to know which files contain what data, ie:

(i)   which files contain the programs. What programs are held on each particular file;

(ii) which files contain certain master file or reference file data, and what files contain transactions data;

(iii) what 'generation' of data is held on a particular file. For example, there might be 3 files for a stock master file, covering 3 generations of data on the 'grandfather-father-son' principle described in an earlier chapter;

(iv) what files are blank or contain data that is not longer needed and so can be overwritten (purged). These files can be used as output files for future processing work;

(v)   what files are 'back-up' files. For data security reasons, it is common to duplicate data on a file by copying it on to another 'back-up' file. If anything goes wrong with the original file, the back-up can be used in its place.

The librarian has the responsibility for keeping the file library, and so keeping a record of the data held on each file. He must also ensure that the data is kept physically secure (eg by locking the door to the file library when he is not in it). Finally, he has the task of sending the files to the computer room when they are needed, and receiving them back again when processing is finished. The data control clerks will tell the librarian what to send, and what data will be contained on the files that come back.

(f) *Computer room supervisor*

The computer room supervisor is responsible for the actual running of the programs on the computer hardware in the computer room. The operations section as a whole has responsibility for:

(i)   carrying out the job specifications received from the job control section;

(ii) getting input and output devices ready (eg magnetic disk drives);

(iii) loading the correct stationery into printers for output;

(iv) loading files for input and output (ie on to the magnetic tape decks and disk drives etc);

(v) keeping a log of all the jobs done;

(vi) in the case of jobs where the operators must feed in extra commands to the computer during processing, the operators will communicate with the CPU via a console. The console includes a typewriter (so that communications from the CPU are kept on record) and a keyboard for inputting instructions;

(vii) maintaining the hardware in good condition (*note:* equipment maintenance and repair work is usually carried out under contract by engineers);

(viii) reporting breakdowns. Calling in engineers to make any repairs to hardware that are needed.

In large computer installations, the computers will be kept operating for 16 and possibly 24 hours a day, and so operators will be divided into two or three shifts, with a shift leader for each shift. A *shift leader* is a senior operator who acts as the supervisor for the shift, in the absence of the computer room supervisor. Each shift leader will have a number of computer operators working for him or her.

62   BASIC REVISION QUESTION: COMPUTER BUREAU

(a) A computer bureau is an organisation providing electronic data processing (EDP) facilities to clients. It will own a range of EDP equipment and employ specialised staff to operate it and to advise clients on the ways in which they might benefit from its use. The bureau's revenue comes from the fees which it charges to clients for the use of its facilities. These may be on a regular basis, eg weekly payroll and/or use on an ad hoc basis, eg processing the results of a market survey.

Types of computer bureaux include:

(i)   independent companies formed to provide this service;
(ii) computer manufacturers with bureaux subsidiaries;
(iii) computer users with spare capacity.

(b) Main advantages are:

(i)   experience of EDP is gained;
(ii)   it may be cheaper than an in-house facility;
(iii) it helps with peak loads;
(iv)   it may provide a stand-by facility;
(v)   it provides expertise for hire;
(vi)   it provides advice on systems development and operation;
(vii) it may provide a fully up-to-date facility;

(viii) it can deal effectively with a one-off application.

Main disadvantages are:

(i)   loss of control over time taken to process data;
(ii)   potential problems in transmission of data;
(iii) bureau may close down leaving customer with no facility;
(iv)   standard of service variable and may not be satisfactory.

63 COMPUTERISED PAYROLL

> *Tutorial note.* When a question asks for an *outline* report, there is no need for you to try to write out a report in full. In any case, you would not have the time, and you would be penalised for not answering the question properly. Just write out the main headings of your report, and summarise very briefly what you would write under each heading.

Title

Computerisation of weekly payroll.

Introduction

Remit of the report, alternatives considered, brief summary of conclusions.

Alternative approaches

(a) *Computer bureau*

    (i)   Description of how system would operate:

        (1) company initiates data;
        (2) data sent to bureau which offers standard payroll processing (possibly including creation of BACS tape);
        (3) bureau returns processed data.

    (ii) Advantages of bureau:

        (1) cost. High capital cost not required;
        (2) expertise. The bureau would not have a learning curve associated with payroll processing;
        (3) minimal effort. The bureau does most of the work, not the company;
        (4) up to date technology. The bureau would constantly be upgrading its hardware/ software because that is its business;
        (5) if the payroll is to be a one-off application, it makes sense to contract it out rather than buy a large computer solely for that purpose.

    (iii) Disadvantages of bureau:

        (1) loss of control over the time taken to process data and in particular the inability to reschedule work should input delays occur;
        (2) problems which may be encountered in the transfer of data to and from the bureau;
        (3) the problems of dealing with error corrections;
        (4) the bureau may close down;

(5) a loss of control (and possibly of security) over an important area;

(6) the standards of service and the provision of adequate documentation control may not be entirely satisfactory.

(b) *Dedicated microcomputer*

    (i)   Description of how the system would operate, ie keyboard input within payroll department.

    (ii)   Advantages of dedicated micro:

        (1) fairly easy to use;

        (2) would not need to 'tie-in' with any other systems;

        (3) fast response time and instant access;

        (4) may be able to get payroll software written especially for the company.

    (iii) Disadvantages of dedicated micro:

        (1) may be security problems;

        (2) may take some time to implement new system;

        (3) software available may not meet all of the company's requirements;

        (4) problems could arise if hardware broke down.

(c) *Custom built system*

    (i)   Description of how the system would operate:

        (1) software written for the company so that;

        (2) the company's main computer could be used to process the payroll.

    (ii)   Advantages of custom built system:

        (1) should meet all needs because it is specifically designed for the company;

        (2) access should not present a problem.

    (iii) Disadvantage of custom built system:

        (1) costly;

        (2) could be problems if in the future the company decides to change its system;

        (3) could be security problems;

        (4) slow implementation;

        (5) continuity of back-up (eg what happens if bugs are found after 3 months, 6 months or a year?).

Costs

Summary of the relevant costs of the various alternatives, identifying common costs.

Conclusions

Recommendations

64   PAYROLL AND BUREAU

> *Tutorial note.* Note that although payroll is probably the data processing application most commonly run by bureaux, it is by no means the only area in which they provide processing facilities.

(a)   *Features of a payroll system*

A payroll application has a specific task to perform (calculating wages and salaries and issuing wage slips).

It is run on a periodic basis (eg weekly, monthly).

Most payroll applications contain similar information, on a payroll master file. This will be made of employee records, one for each employee.

- Each employee has an employee number, which is often the key field on the record.
- Other standing details (the employee's name, tax code, rate of pay) are included.
- The payroll contains information brought forward from previous periods, in particular gross pay, tax paid to date, National Insurance paid to date, net pay to date.
- Current period basic pay, overtime, total gross pay, sick pay tax, National Insurance and other deductions.

Inputs to a normal payroll system include the following.

- Gross annual salaries (for salaried staff).
- Time sheets (for hourly-paid staff).
- Hourly pay rates.
- Tax rates.
- National Insurance Rates.
- Amendments to standing data (eg joiners and leavers, for file maintenance).

Outputs from a typical payroll application include the following.

- Pay slips.
- Tax forms (eg P60).
- Wages analysis by department.
- Payroll printout.
- A magnetic tape for use in the BACS system (so that funds are transferred electronically from employers' to employees' bank accounts.)

(b)   *Activities of a computer bureau*

A computer bureau provides a variety of computer services to customers. A computer bureau might run whole applications, or simply provide computer time to users to employ as they choose.

The range of services offered by computer bureaux is considerable, with some offering a complete service while others specialise in particular areas. The services offered include the following.

(i)   *Data preparation.* Transcribing data from source documents into a machine readable form (eg on to magnetic tape/disks etc), including the services offered for file conversion on system implementation.

(ii) *Hiring computer time.* The bureau will process the clients' data on its own computer. The client may be responsible for providing the programs, but many bureaux offer application packages (eg for payroll).

(iii) *Do-it-yourself.* The bureau will provide the computer but the client will provide operators, programs etc. This type of service may be provided by computer users with spare capacity in off-peak periods.

(iv) *Consultancy.* The bureau will provide advice and assistance in connection with feasibility studies, system design, equipment evaluation, staff training etc.

(v) *Software.* The bureau will design, write, test and provide software for a particular application; or may design and/or adapt application packages.

(vi) *Time-sharing/remote job entry (RJE).* The client uses his own terminal(s) (linked by a data transmission method) to process data on the bureau computer. As business data processing usually involves large volumes of data input/output, the terminals must be powerful and fast enough to deal with the data efficiently.

(vii) *Turnkey operation.* Where the bureau undertakes the client's conversion to a computer system. For example, a computer bureau may be engaged to carry out the feasibility study, order the computer hardware from a supplier and supervise its installation, do all the systems design work, write (or adapt) application programs and test the programs and the system. When the system is complete in every detail and working perfectly it is handed over to the client. All the client has to do is 'turn the key' to commence using the system.

(c) The bureau accepts a batch (or batches) of transactions from the client, processes it (or them) and sends the printed outputs to the client. In this case the bureau will also hold standing data for each employee. Monthly data necessary to process the payroll will be transmitted from the terminal over the link to the bureau. The bureau will process the data and produce wages/salary slips, a wages analysis and any other information the client needs. The client will receive the output within a stipulated turn-round time so that wages processing is not delayed.

65 INSTALLATION AND RUNNING COSTS

> *Tutorial note.* The question wording specifically excludes hardware and software costs and you would receive little credit for writing about these.

Installation costs

- Set-up of computer room, if necessary.

- Electric cabling.

- In older buildings, the adaptations to a building necessary to cope with electric cabling can be considerable (eg false ceilings).

- Generators in case of power cuts.

- New system documentation.

- Training of user staff.

- Provision of support (always necessary, but greater when a system is new).

- Physical security of computer, and magnetic storage media (eg safes).

- Redundancy payments, if necessary.

Running costs

- Storage media (eg floppy disks).

- Maintenance of backup facilities.

- Salaries of data processing staff.

- Insurance premiums.

- Maintenance contracts payments.

- Regular staff training.

- Data transmission costs (eg line rentals).

(*Tutorial note*: only *five* examples of each type of cost were required).

66 ASSESSING A DP PROJECT

(a) The introduction of a new computerised system can involve major changes in the departments' organisation and it is necessary that a careful study should be made of alternative systems with senior management taking an active interest in the selection process.

A company with a large data processing department would probably use a feasibility team to do the detailed work of a feasibility study. Such a study would assess the advantages and disadvantages of the proposed system from the technical, economic, social and organisational points of view. The feasibility team would produce a report which would include a plan for the development, implementation and control of the proposed scheme. This report would be presented to a steering committee which would normally include representations of top management from the department affected by the proposed computer system. The steering committee has a responsibility to assess the costs and benefits of a new project and would approve or reject the project, or submit its recommendations to the board of directors should their approval be required.

(b) The systems and programming manager has the responsibility for overseeing the development of new programs and systems. His tasks would include:

(i) planning the development of new computer projects;
(ii) managing the staff who:
  (1) carry out the development work;
  (2) maintain and update existing systems and programs;
  (3) test new systems once they are installed;
(iii) ensuring development projects are completed on time;
(iv) arranging technical training;
(v) assisting in recruitment of staff for systems analysis or programming work;
(vi) liaising between programming staff and systems analysis staff.

67 BASIC REVISION QUESTION: RISKS AND CONTROLS

(a) Data and information can suffer for a number of reasons relating to the physical, organisational and technical environment in which they are held.

These can be summarised as follows.

Human error (eg incorrectly entering transactions)
Technical error (eg hardware malfunction)
Natural disasters (eg fire)
Deliberate actions (eg fraud)
Commercial espionage
Malicious damage (sabotage, deliberate introduction of a computer virus)
Industrial action

(b) (i) General controls relate to the environment in which computer systems are developed, maintained and operated.

An example is the proper use of back-up facilities, or authorisation controls over systems development.

(ii) Application controls are specific to each application. They relate to ensuring the completeness and accuracy of the records and the valid entry and processing. They include data validation checks.

68 CONTROLS OVER INPUT AND STORED DATA

(a) (i) *Controls over computer input via a visual display unit*

The objectives of control over the input of data via a visual display unit are threefold:

● to protect against the entering of unauthorised input;
● to ensure complete processing of input data;
● to ensure accurate processing of input data.

(1) *Controls over access.* Particularly with on-line and real-time systems there must be a combination of physical and software or programmed controls to prevent unauthorised personnel from making input via a VDU terminal:

● use of passwords: systems software is programmed to accept inputs only upon entry of an acceptable password. The passwords are protected by periodic changes and careful control over their issue and recording;

● physical access controls: these may be exercised both by controlling access to rooms where a VDU is situated and by the use of keys or badges to use a terminal or even for particular applicants once on a terminal. Careful control must be exercised over the issue of badges.

(2) *Controls over completeness of input.* These include:

- use of batch control totals with manual and programmed agreement following processing of input;

- use of pre-numbering and programmed sequence checking;

- strict controls over rejected and re-submitted input;

- one for one checking of output to hard copy input;

- use of systems software to match inputs to a control file containing expected inputs;

- document counts.

(3) *Controls over accuracy of input.* These include:

- check digit verifications using systems software;
- reasonableness checks using systems software;
- existence tests against known codes;
- one for one checking;
- use of clear, easily read documents.

In addition, control is aided by the use of 'user friendly' software allowing the operator to test input of individual transactions before progressing to updating of files. All the above controls will be strengthened by effective training and good manuals.

(ii) *Controls over computer processing*

These control objectives are to ensure:

- all input data is processed;
- each transaction is accurately processed;
- the appropriate files are used for processing;
- all updating is complete and accurate;
- all output produced is complete and accurate.

(1) *Application controls.* These include:

- batch reconciliation printed after updating;

- use of document counts;

- run to run controls automatically accumulating and reconciling control totals from input through each processing stage. This would be effected by systems software and totals would be held on file for subsequent use;

- use of header labels to identify files used in processing;

- file security arrangements to ensure correct generation of file used in processing;

- printouts of all master file amendments processed;

- use of checkpoints to dump complete contents of store during lengthy processing runs.

(2) *General controls.* These fall into the following categories:

- effective segregation of duties between operational processing and other functions

- effective training and good manuals;

- effective set-up and execution procedures.

(b) *The objectives and methods of control over stored data*

The control objectives are to ensure:

- complete, accurate and authorised amendments;
- complete and accurate updating;
- continued integrity of master files and reference files.

Controls would include the following.

(i) *Application controls.* Methods available include:

- dumping and cyclical checking by the user departments, perhaps on a one for one basis of all stored data to security copies;

- maintenance of control totals by value and last total stored on master files to be checked whenever processing takes place;

- user identification of files by the use of file labels to be read by the operator and the computer;

- printing out of all amendments for independent review and checking for authorisation;

- periodic file re-organisation;

- regular dumping and the creation of security copies;

- use of generation technique of three cycle security copies for data stored on magnetic tape.

(ii) *General controls.* These fall into the following categories:

- segregation of duties between operators and file library functions;

- physical controls over security and operational files;

- effective training and procedure manuals;

- adequate disaster recovery procedures to ensure rapid use of relatively recent security copies.

69 BATCH CONTROL SYSTEM

Ten measures which should be included in a successful batch control system are as follows.

(a) Source documents should be manually checked for validity and authorisation before being processed.

(b) Batch controls should be established when a sufficient number of related documents are gathered together (into a batch). Batch control slip data includes:

    (i)   batch number;
    (ii) computer system identification code;
    (iii) various control totals; and
    (iv) authorisation.

(c) Batch control details are noted both in the data preparation department and in the data processing department, whenever a batch leaves or arrives at a department. This affords a cross-check to ensure that no data goes missing (and is not missed) in between departments.

(d) Data is *verified* when keyed in (to ensure there are no transcription errors).

(e) Data is *validated* as it is input to the computer (ie the computer will reject any obviously incorrect data as specified by its data vet program.).

(f) Accepted and rejected data is reconciled to batch control totals to ensure all data has been passed into the computer.

(g) After valid data has been processed, the computer again prints out control totals which should be compared with batch control totals (either manually, or by the computer, or by a combination of both).

(h) All rejected transaction records should be carefully investigated and followed up (and not forgotten).

(i) Output should be sent to the right user department at the right time - possibly by reference to a standard checklist.

(j) Backup copies of computer discs or tapes should be kept so that data can be recreated in the event of some major disaster.

70 DATA CONTROL

> *Tutorial note* . You will find that terms like these are really not too complicated if you can provide an example of each. A definition of a validation report or a reconciliation check can be pretty bare without some sort of description of an application to bring it to life.

(a) *Check digit*

Check digits are used in data validation. A check digit is a character added to the end of a code number which is to be input to a computer for processing. Check digits are normally used in conjunction with the more important items of data such as account numbers.

A formula is used to generate a check digit by reference to the characters in the code number itself. If the code number is input incorrectly, the chances of the check digit generated passing the same formula test are very low - a different number, containing for example a transposition error, would generate a *different* check digit.

A common system of check digits is the *Modulus 11* system. This multiplies each digit of the code by a different weighted factor and the resulting products are added together. The check digit is added to give a total which is exactly divisible by 11.

(b) *Validation report*

A validation report may be generated after data has been entered and subjected to validation checks. There are two types of validation report. The first is a *rejection report*. This shows records which cannot be processed further. A rejection report may show records which have not been processed because the account number check digits do not balance.

The second in an *exception report*. This shows records which have been processed but which do not fall within the range or limit specified by a particular test. The fact that records do not satisfy a test does not automatically mean that they are invalid, and therefore the processing takes place, but it is important that all items highlighted in this way are followed up.

(c) *Reconciliation check*

A reconciliation check is a check which compares two sets of data. Typically the two sets of data would be data input to a process and data output from the same process. A reconciliation check focuses on the quantity of transactions input and the financial value of those transactions. If the quantity of transactions and their total value after processing is unchanged, then assurance is obtained that the processing run has successfully processed each transaction.

If the quantity and value processed is lower than that input, it may be that some items have been rejected and so the rejection report may form a reconciling item. Alternatively an unreconcilable difference may indicate that some items were not input at all (eg a batch may have been omitted).

(d) *File header*

A file header is a special record stored with a file of ordinary records. It appears at the start of a file, whether on tape or disk, and provides important control details relevant to the file. These control details include:

(i) name of file
(ii) date of creation of file
(iii) file reference number
(iv) file size

and other relevant data such as the file's purge date. The file header is designed to ensure that any processing is performed on the right file. Thus if a grandfather-father-son technique of back-ups is used, the file header will correctly identify the 'son' as being the version to be used for an update run. Similarly the 'grandfather' will only be purged once the purge date is reached.

(e) *Update error*

An update error occurs when data which has been successfully validated cannot be processed. This may occur for a number of reasons.

If a data item has been entered with a customer code which is in the right format (eg AAANNN) but there is no corresponding code on the master file, the transaction cannot be processed. This is an update error and would appear as such on a rejection or error report generated after the processing run is completed.

71 BASIC REVISION QUESTION: SECURITY

(a) The *grandfather, father, son technique* of reconstructing magnetic tape files means keeping as many generations of historical master files, transaction files and reference files as is considered necessary for the security of both the files and the data contained on them. It is common to keep three generations (grandfather, father and son) of master files, and sufficient transaction files to re-create the father from the grandfather master file. The 'elder' files should be kept at a different location.

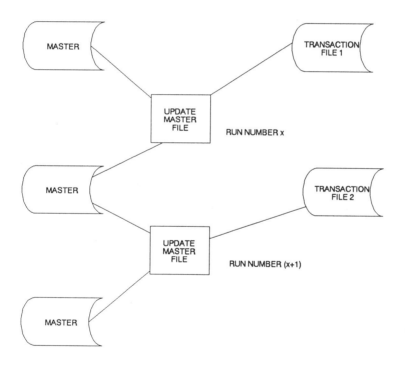

If the 'son' tape out of run number (x + 1) is found to contain corrupted data, a corrected master file can be recreated by going back to the generation 2 master file (the 'father') and the associated transaction file and carrying out run number (x + 1) again.

(b) *Passwords* are a form of software control. Passwords can be applied to data files, program files and to *parts* of a program. The British Computer Society's definition of a password is 'a sequence of characters which must be presented to a computer system before it will allow access to the system of parts of that system (eg a particular file)'. An example of a password is the personal identification number (PIN) with cash cards for bank or building society cash dispensers. The cash dispenser checks the PIN code on the magnetic strip of the cash card against the code number keyed in by the cardholder, and the two codes must match before the cardholder is allowed to withdraw any cash.

72 PHYSICAL SECURITY

The consequences of losing data held on magnetic storage media or of being unable to process that data due to physical damage to the computer hardware can be disastrous for a company. It is therefore essential that all computer installations have adequate physical security. The main physical risks and the steps necessary to minimise these are detailed below.

(a) *Fire, flood or other natural disaster*
The risk from fire is normally minimised by having adequate fire detection systems in the computer area and appropriate fire suppression apparatus, eg sprinklers. Data files should always be stored in fireproof safes. Back up copies of programs and data files should be held at a remote location normally in a separate building. Arrangements should be made to run essential processing at alternative computer facilities should a catastrophe prevent processing at the company's site.

(b) *Dust, humidity, temperature*
Many larger computers are very sensitive to these factors. It is therefore essential that the computer environment is properly controlled. Measures to minimise these risks include antistatic carpets, special access arrangements to prevent air flow from outside the computer area and air conditioning to control humidity and air temperature.

(c) *Power failure*
Computers are dependent, obviously, on a constant supply of electricity. They can also be damaged by unpredictable power surges which may cause corruption of data. Most large installations have alternative power generator facilities and systems which ensure the maintenance of a constant power supply.

(d) *Magnetic interference*
The contents of magnetic storage media can be damaged when the tapes or disks are in close proximity to other sources of magnetism. Therefore magnetic files should not be stored close to machinery, particularly if it is powered by electronic motors, or to other equipment which might cause data to be corrupted.

(e) *Unauthorised access*
Computer installations are vulnerable to people wishing to inflict damage on the company, be it for criminal intent or simply the revenge of a disgruntled employee or competitor. Good physical security is therefore essential. Normal security measures, including security personnel, access passes for staff and visitors on the company building, should be supplemented by access controls on the computer area itself. These may include access codes, machine readable cards, thumb prints etc. In addition the data library should also have access controls over it. Access to terminals should be controlled through logs, password controls, etc.

73 MINIMISE RISKS

There are many threats to data and computer systems, and they can be divided into two main areas.

- Threats of a purely physical/environmental nature: in some cases the *possibility* that the threat might be realised can be minimised; in others, an organisation can only minimise the *effect* of the realised threat.

- Threats relating to human operation of the system from human error or deliberate damage.

Natural disasters. Little can be done to prevent their occurrence, but organisations can take some measures to reduce their impact:

- data is backed up regularly for storage elsewhere;

- a back up *system* is available;

- in the case of flooding, computer systems should not be installed in the basement of a flood risk area;

- in the case of other natural disasters (eg earthquakes), strict building regulations should be enforced.

Fire. The threat of fire to data can be minimised if (1) measures are taken to minimise the likelihood of fire breaking out in the first place and (2) other measures are taken to ensure that if a fire does occur the damage it causes is restricted:

- fire detection devices should be used;

- fire regulations should be followed (eg fire doors);

- the organisation has a fire prevention policy, which is actively enforced (eg regulations regarding smoking in the computer room);

- smoking is restricted;

- data is backed up regularly for storage elsewhere;

- fire-proof safes are used for floppy disk, tape storage;

- a backup system is available.

Other threats relating to the system's controllable physical environment

Physical damage to equipment: can be minimised if proper safeguards and procedures are instituted and exercised (eg separate computer room, air conditioning, no overcrowding etc). Also portable storage media (eg floppy disks) should not be left lying around where they might be damaged.

Power failure: alternative sources of power should be available to take over in case of power failure, so that processing can continue without loss of data. The backup source should be activated as soon as the power fails.

Threats to data and systems arising from the human environment include the following.

Theft/terrorism: security measures to control access to equipment and/or data stores (eg security passes, video monitors etc).

Hacking: unauthorised access to computer systems. Can be checked by rigorous use of *passwords,* and a security-conscious strategy to software and network design, and systems operation.

Viruses: computer programs that attach themselves to other programs and act when the host program is run. Typical means of entry into a system is the use of an infected floppy disk (eg with pirated material). If the infected computer is part of a network, the virus can be passed easily from machine to machine. Viruses can be countered by some virus protection programs.

Human error at programming stage: this can be minimised if program specifications are sufficiently precise to avoid ambiguity, and if testing is rigorous. Bugs may be a result of errors. Proper program design (eg modular programming) may reduce this risk. All program amendments must be authorised, checked and validated before use.

Human error in operating the system: a variety of controls exist to minimise this risk, eg data validation routines, control total reconciliation. However, in some applications, such as spreadsheets, it may be necessary to examine the model to ensure that it is accurate.

Fraud: some form of segregation of duties may be necessary to reduce the possibility of fraud, but this does not rule out collusion between members of staff with different functions.

74   INTERNAL CONTROL IN A DP SYSTEM

(a)   There are a number of alternatives:

    (i)   the data on purchase invoices could be transcribed onto special input forms designed to suit in-house needs; or

    (ii)   since it is likely that the purchase invoice details will need to be vouched to purchase order details anyway, purchase invoice details could be transcribed onto copy purchase order forms, which will contain suitable spaces for prices, VAT, discount terms etc; or

    (iii)   the problem could be ignored altogether with the result that the operator must search through each individual purchase invoice to find the data required; this requires a high degree of skill and attentiveness on the part of the operator in order to avoid (say) confusing delivery date with invoice date.

(b)   Verification is the process by which, at the point of input, the computer operator ensures that the data input into the computer is the same as the data available on source documents. In contrast to validation, verification makes no attempt to discover whether the data input is actually correct; it merely determines the correctness of transcription.

    There are two methods of verification available when using a VDU screen:

    (i)   the data input will be displayed on the screen during input; after a screen has been filled, the operator can read through the text and compare it with the source document(s). If it appears satisfactory, it can then be released from the VDU's own memory into the mainframe;

    (ii)   alternatively, input data could be processed against copy masterfiles and the transactions and results kept in suspense until verified by a supervisor. Once everything has been verified satisfactorily, the transactions data can be processed against actual master files.

(c)   Validation describes a range of software routines designed to ensure that errors contained in a source document or file are detected. Naturally, data validation cannot form a comprehensive check on errors, since a computer can only detect errors which are obviously implausible (eg the use of non-existent code-numbers); incorrect data which is nonetheless plausible will not be detected. Validation routines are usually the first programs to be operated in any processing run.

The main types of data validation checks are discussed below:

    (i)   *Range checks*
These are designed to ensure that data in a certain field lies within predetermined limits. A range check in this example might be used to highlight possible pricing errors; the computer would match unit prices with a reference file of suppliers' price lists and print out a list of prices which deviated from the list price by ±5%.

    (ii)   *Limit checks*
These checks are similar to range checks and check that data is not below a certain value or above a certain value. In this example, a limit check might cause all purchase invoices with a net value of greater than £200,000 to be listed on an exception report and all those with a net value greater than £500,000 to be rejected altogether.

    (iii)   *Existence checks*
These ensure that data in a particular field is valid for that field. In this example existence checks might be used to ensure that:

- a quoted stock number is valid by comparing it with an on-line reference file;

- a quoted purchase order number is valid by comparing it with an on-line master file of purchase orders;

- all details contained on an invoice agree with details on the relevant purchase orders.

    (iv)   *Format checks*
These ensure that the data contained in a field are in an appropriate format, eg that a field which is intended to contain numeric data is of the correct size, is not left blank and does not contain letters or combinations of letters and numbers. In this example, such a check could be used to ensure that fields which should contain monetary data do actually contain numbers.

    (v)   *Combination checks*
These are essentially calculation checks. For example, if a purchase invoice has a net value of £100 and VAT is set at 15%, the computer will ensure that the gross value given is £115 and not some other figure.

    (vi)   *Check digit verification*
Check digits are added to code numbers to reduce the chances of transcription and transposition errors. The computer will perform calculations on the code numbers to detect any such errors.

(d) The final computer report can be divided into a number of parts:

(i) Transactions details:

(1) Purchase orders. The report should contain a list of orders processed, including the following details:
- purchase order numbers
- date of order
- stock numbers
- authorisation codes
- values or orders
- supplier names
- supplier codes.

(2) Purchase invoices. All purchase invoices processed must be listed, including the following details:
- internal purchase invoice numbers
- suppliers' invoice reference numbers
- invoice date
- relevant purchase order numbers
- stock numbers
- authorisation codes
- supplier names
- supplier codes
- account codes
- payment dates.

(ii) Other details:

(1) The report should list:

- all those orders and invoices which have been rejected after failing validation checks (the error report), with an indication of the nature of the error;

- all those orders and invoices which, although failing validation checks, have been accepted for processing (the exception report), with an indication of the nature of the problem.

(2) Additionally, the report should provide the following information:

- the date of the report
- control totals to allow manual reconciliation by the purchasing department
- a list of invoices now due for payment
- a list of purchase invoices for which no delivery has been received
- a list of purchase orders for which no invoice has been received
- historical data giving total orders and payments made for the financial year to date, broken down by supplier, stock type etc.

(e) The following controls are required:

(i) Security. Since the system is on-line, with direct access to master files, security is a particular problem. It is necessary to prevent unauthorised access to VDUs, in the ways indicated below:

(1)   physical security: rooms containing terminals should be kept locked when not in use;

(2)   passwords: each operator should be given a secret password which must be input before the VDU can accept data;

(3)   menu restriction: terminal users can be restricted to the use of certain files and programs.

(ii) Other controls:

(1)   batching: in spite of being on-line, batch processing routines should still be maintained (this does not appear to be a real-time system); batch preparation and reconciliation can be performed at the end of the day. Batch totals could include the total number of invoices processed and hash totals of invoice numbers, purchase order numbers etc;

(2)   dumping: it will be necessary for the contents of on-line files to be dumped periodically so that, if a VDU operator accidentally causes erasure of master or transaction files, there remain back-up files which are reasonably up to date;

(3)   referencing: a clear system of cross-referencing between computer information and source documentation will facilitate the detection of error.

(*Tutorial note*: although the question requires only four parts to be answered, all five parts are considered above, for the sake of completeness.)

75 TEN CONTROLS

> *Tutorial note*. There is a vast number of controls which you could have listed in answer to this question. It was not clear how detailed your answer should have been.

The successful functioning of an organisation's information systems is an important factor in its success. Breakdown of an organisation's data processing can result in massive financial loss. Computer systems are also prone to sophisticated fraud.

It is possible to identify two types of control.

General controls relate to the environment within which computer-based systems are developed, maintained and operated and are generally applicable to all the applications.

Controls over the systems environment include the following.

●   Personnel recruitment policies to ensure honesty and competence of employees.

●   Segregation of duties between different types of job, to minimise tampering with programs and/or data.

●   Proper training programs for new staff and for new systems developments.

●   Physical security of hardware and software. This includes basic security procedures, restricted entry to the computer room, the existence and operation of an organisation-wide security policy.

Controls over systems development include the following.

- Authorisation procedures for development project (eg by steering committee, or senior management if over a certain amount).

- Proper system justification in cost and operational terms.

- Proper control over the actual process of system development, using various project management techniques.

- Regular review of work on a project completed to date.

- Use, perhaps, of a systems development methodology to provide uniformity of documents, and to ensure that user requirements are specified in detail in advance and agreed by users.

- Controls to ensure all systems are tested before implementation.

- Controls over changes to systems (eg approval, documentation).

Controls over system maintenance include the following.

- Controls to ensure regular reviews of system performance, follow up of any bugs, and so forth.

- Authorisation procedures for program amendments and testing.

Controls over systems operation include the following.

- Basic physical security against natural disasters or thefts.

- Backup procedures (eg maintaining copies of files off-site, arranging an emergency source of processing power).

- Controls over access to the system (eg passwords to prevent unauthorised individuals having access to files).

- Controls over hardware usage (eg a policy requiring every floppy disk from an outsider to be run through an anti-virus procedure to limit the chance of infection).

- Controls over access to data files (eg locks on the library door, passwords).

- Segregation of program files and data files.

- Controls over humidity and temperature (especially for mainframe applications).

- Measures to ensure the system is not accessed during data transmission (eg by a hacker).

- Controls to ensure that the computing resources are used efficiently (eg very bulky processing runs to take place over night to free the system for use during the day).

Application controls are those specific to each application.

- Controls over input (eg verification, batch control totals, validation and data vet routines, review of input data).

- Controls over processing (eg checkpoint programs, recovery procedures, file identification checks, regular review of master file data).

- Controls over output (eg distribution, actioning of error reports, maintenance of audit trail).

- Controls over data (eg a coding system).

76 SYSTEM SPECIFICATION

(a) The system specification is the authoritative document for the development and implementation of a computer system. It acts as a reference document for any future alterations. It is the analysts' means of communicating with:

- management (for final approval);
- programmers;
- operations staff (detail all operating procedures);
- user departments;
- auditors.

(b) A typical specification would contain the sections outlined below.

Section A - Introductory information

(i) Title, responsibilities
(ii) Index
(iii) Glossary of terms used
(iv) Timetable for installation
(v) Details of amendments

Section B - Objectives of the system

(i) Procedures covered
(ii) Departments concerned
(iii) Measures of effectiveness

Section C - Description of the system

(i) Clerical procedures
(ii) Data preparation
(iii) Output distribution
(iv) Computer procedures, with run charts

Section D - Detailed specifications

(i)   Files: medium, size, contents
              storage media

(ii)   Input specification: frequency of input
                             method
                             specimen copies

(iii) Output specification: medium
                              distribution
                              specimens
                              parameters for designing new outputs

Section E - Program specification

(i)   This will contain details of the exact requirements of each program. Programmers will use this as a set of instructions.

Section F - Equipment

(i)   Type of computer and peripherals
(ii)   Frequency of utilisation of computer and peripherals

Section G - Test data

Section H - Changeover procedures

(i)   Conversion of files: methods
                            codings
(ii)   Pilot running/parallel running.

77 PROCEDURES MANUAL

> *Tutorial note.* In his comments on the examination, the examiner noted that this was by some distance the worst answered question on the paper. This stemmed from a failure to read the question, which asks candidates to *list* and *briefly explain* the *sections* of a manual. Some candidates explained purchase ledger systems and others wrote essays about manuals, but few answered the question.

A key to successful systems implementation and operation is appropriate user documentation, whose functions include:

(a)   assisting training of users at systems changeover;
(b)   provision of a first port of call for any difficulties or queries users might have;
(c)   training of new members of staff when they join.

A *procedures manual* is documentation relating to the day to day operation of the system from the user's point of view. It will contain both instructions as to how the system is operated, and also controls relating to its operation which may be enforced by disciplinary sanction. The procedures manual may be updated regularly.

A procedures manual will typically include the following.

(1) Title and contents page, with date of issue.

(2) Distribution list.

(3) Overall controls eg:

- specific injunction not to share passwords;
- rules governing access to computer room;
- rules governing access to library, and library procedures;
- what to do in case of system breakdown;
- number of people required to be present in computer room when some applications are run;
- rules relating to backup (eg all microcomputer resident hard disks to be backed up on tape at the end of each day).

(4) Outline description of system: interrelationship between different system modules.

(5) For each individual system module:

- simple case study for demonstration purposes;
- entry procedures, and a hierarchical picture of menu if a menu-driven system;
- input documents;
- common processing tasks, with specimen screen formats at each stage;
- explanation of error messages, and how to deal with them;
- printed outputs.

78 DATA PROCESSING STANDARDS MANUAL

> *Tutorial note.* Data processing standards are an important concept. You should ensure that you do not confuse the manual referred to here with a procedures manual. You were only required to describe the contents of *four* of the sections of the manual.

(a) A manual should minimise the likelihood of errors and misunderstanding.

(i) It should apply to all tasks within a DP department:

1 documentation;
2 operations;
3 authority to approve activities.

(ii) The manual should be distributed to all relevant staff, such as:

1 management;
2 analysts;
3 programmers;
4 operators;
5 user departments.

(iii)   The main purposes of the manual are:

1   to provide a good understanding of the system;
2   to record the standards and measure performance against those standards;
3   to reduce the problems of staff (if a programmer moves on all is not lost);
4   to communicate effectively (eg a systems analyst must make his design intentions perfectly clear to the programmer in his program specification; a programmer must provide full documentation of his program so that amendments to the program or corrections of errors can be made more easily.
5   to tell computer and clerical staff how to operate the system.

(b)   A data processing standards manual which might typically have the following contents.

DATA PROCESSING STANDARDS MANUAL

Section

1   *Introduction*

Statement of policy with regard to standards, contents, purpose of the manual.

2   *Management*

Role of the Steering Committee.
Information Centre terms of reference.
The programme of meetings (both within the department and with user department management).
Planning and control of projects.
Budgets.
Costing.
Performance standards.
The management organisation (eg organisation chart).
Job specification for all staff.
Staff recruitment and training.
Management reports.

3   *Systems analysis standards*

Introductory information.
Methodology.
Diagramming conventions.
System objectives.
Systems description.
Changeover procedure.
Equipment.
Output specification.
Input specification.
File specification.
Test data.
Program description.
System operating details.

4   *Programming standards*

Methods of work:

- program structuring (and flowcharting)
- coding
- programs testing and amendment
- instructions to operators for each program.

5   *Operating standards*

Console operating methods.
Peripheral equipment operating methods.
Computer room security.
File library procedures.

6   *Documentation*

The system of documenting DP work should also be standardised. In other words, there should be standard documents as well as standard information contained in the documents.

7   *Specification of computer configuration*

CPU.
Peripheral equipment in the computer room.
Remote terminals.
Network hardware.
Network software.

79   DP TERMS

(a)   *Kimball tags v point of sale terminals*

A computer input medium commonly associated with clothes shops is a punched tag (Kimball tag) containing information about the particular item, eg stock number, size, price. The tags are attached to the garment when it is displayed and removed when it is sold (the point of 'data capture'). They will normally be converted to another input medium, eg magnetic tape, before input.

More and more large retail stores are introducing electronic point of sale devices which act as cash registers, but are also terminals connected to a main computer. This enables the computer to produce useful management information such as sales details and analysis and stock control information very quickly. Some systems on the market use wands or laser scanners to read optical characters (or bar codes) on the product package, so eliminating keying-in errors by the sales operative. Other systems use keyboard input, with the person on the cash desk keying in data from a sales ticket or label on the item being sold, although the sales price is not keyed in. Product prices are looked up on a master file (eg using the bar coded product codes) and the sales details are used to update all relevant files, such as stock file and sales analysis file. A fully itemised, accurate and descriptive receipt can be produced for the customer, who will also feel the benefit of faster moving queues at the checkout. Management will obtain more information more quickly than was ever possible before, and the computer can monitor stock levels and reorder stocks automatically.

(b) *Indexed sequential files v random access files*

Indexed sequential: records are held in key field sequence, but are addressable by means of an *index* which is held as data on part of the disk. Only master files or reference files are likely to be organised indexed sequentially, while transaction files will be organised serially or sequentially. Files with an index can be processed by means of direct access; ie the computer can go straight to the record which is to be read into the CPU or can write new records directly at an address location of the file.

Random: a randomly organised file contains records stored without regard to the sequence of their control (key) fields. Records are loaded in any convenient sequence and are then retrieved by establishing a direct relationship between the key of the record and its address on the file, either by use of an index or by manipulation of the key itself (this is known as 'address generation'). Randomly organised files show distinct advantages where:

(i)   the hit rate is low;
(ii)   data cannot be conveniently batched or sorted;
(iii)   a fast response is required.

Random organisation is a commonly used method in real time systems.

(c) *File dumping v file purging*

Dumping is the process by which the contents of external storage are copied on to a computer file. It is performed in the following situations:

(i)   the commonest means of providing back-up copies of disk files is to copy (dump) the contents of disks on to spare media (often magnetic tapes); this might be done every evening. These back-up disks or tapes will then be stored away from active disks;

(ii)   in on-line processing systems, where operators have direct access to master files, it is prudent to make frequent copies of master files in case they become corrupted during the day's processing.

Purging is the process by which the entire contents of a tape or disk are erased. This will occur when the data contained has become out-of-date and there are more up-to-date versions available. Once purged the file can be used to hold fresh data. Both tapes and disks contain data about their 'purge date' in their internal labels: any instruction to the computer to purge a file on a date before the given purge date will be ignored by the computer.

80 EXPLAIN AND ILLUSTRATE

(a) A *turnround document* is a document which is initially produced by the computer. It is then used to collect more data and re-input to the computer for processing.

Examples of turn round documents are:

(i)   the payment counterfoil on many bills which are sent out periodically to customers - eg gas bills, electricity bills, telephone bills, credit card bills. Usually such bills are examples of turnround documents making use of optical character recognition (OCR), where the computer reads stylised characters by light sensing methods;

(ii) multiple choice examination papers. The computer produces the exam papers, including boxes for the students to tick to indicate their answers. The completed exam papers are fed back into the computer, which detects where the ticks are and marks the papers accordingly. This is an example of turnround documents making use of optical mark reading (OMR), where the computer detects lines or crosses, again by specialised lighting techniques.

The advantages of turnround documents are:

(1) they improve the accuracy of data, because much of it is computer-produced. Only a few items need to be added later to the computer-produced document in order to complete the data capture;

(2) they increase the speed of data capture;

(3) they reduce the need for verification checks and validation checks of data input;

(4) they are cheap to produce and use.

The main drawback to turnround documents is their limited application. There are not many situations where an organisation can produce a document which can then be used for subsequent data input.

(b) *Exception reporting,* or *reporting by exception*, means that instead of producing a great amount of rather boring information which all looks rather similar, only information on something different or unusual is produced. People are only informed about the *exceptions* to normal practice, which is why it is called the exception principle or reporting by exception.

For example, suppose the managing director of a firm decided to keep a strict eye on staff timekeeping and staff absences. He would not thank his personnel officers if, each week, they provided him with statistics on *every* member of staff. Most members of staff, after all, will come to work regularly and on time. What the managing director wants is an exception report, detailing the exceptions to the norm. In this case, the managing director would require a shortlist of staff who are late for work, and another list of staff who are repeatedly absent.

81 SUNDRY TERMS

Tutorial note. With the possible exception of part (b) any of these terms could feature in a question worth 10 or 12 marks, and so you should have had plenty of material to draw on in writing answers here.

(a) *Minicomputer*

The distinction between mainframe, mini- and micro-computer is one derived from the history of computers. A minicomputer was so called in contrast to a mainframe computer, as it was not so powerful having a smaller memory and shorter word length. The distinction between a minicomputer and a microcomputer is rather vague. Microcomputers have traditionally been used for personal computing only (ie only supported one user) and had limited processing power.

However, the distinction between microcomputers and minicomputers is disappearing, as microprocessor chips become more powerful.

(b) *Viewdata*

Viewdata is the 'generic term applied to systems which provide information through a telephone network to a television or terminal screen'. (CIMA *Computing Technology.*) The user is connected to the system by telephone link, and uses a keypad to access or send information through the system via the telephone unit.

The most important feature of viewdata, that makes it difficult from teletext, is that it is *interactive* - in other words, a viewdata customer can transmit information through the viewdata network as well as receive it. Some companies transmit information to their branches in this way.

Viewdata can be used to provide an electronic mail system, with the messages being sent via the viewdata system and appearing on the recipient's viewdata (TV) screen.

Viewdata can also be used, like teletext, to 'call up' information from a remote database, and displayed on a TV-type screen at the specific request of the user.

In the UK the viewdata service is provided by British Telecom and called Prestel. In the Prestel service most of the information is paid for by organisations that wish to provide the information. The Prestel service is provided over the telephone system, and so throughout the time he is connected to it, the user must pay for the 'telephone call', at normal call rates. In addition, the user must pay a fee for consulting most pages of information (but not index pages and some other pages). This fee is paid to British Telecom, which then passes it on, less commission, to the information provider.

(c) *Network*

A network is a collection of computers and other equipment linked together either by special cable, or over the telecommunications network, or both. Data can be sent from computer to computer or from computer to peripheral device.

The processors and peripheral devices in a local area network (LAN) are linked by special cable and as a consequence are found within a small geographical distance from each other (eg in the same building). Special network software is often required to enable the computers to speak to each other. A network enables several micros to share one printer for example.

A wide area network (WAN) is connected over the telecommunications system.

A network can be configured in a number of ways. Some networks may use a central computer as the repository of all the data and program files (a file server). In other cases, programs and data files may be distributed widely over the network. Networks are necessary for the implementation of electronic mail and other features of the electronic office.

(d) *Database*

A database is a collection of data. The organisation of the data in a database file is not determined by the uses to which the data is put (ie the applications). So, one set of data can be used by a variety of application programs.

The organisation of the database, and the connection with the applications, is provided by a piece of software called the database management system (DBMS).

Users access the database in a number of ways. A data manipulation language is used for hierarchical and network databases, and a query language for relational databases.

(e) *Application package*

An application package is a type of software. It is a set of programs designed for a particular programs and sold as a whole. An application package is often designed by a software house, and sold to a number of different companies. Many organisations find the use of applications packages a cheap alternative to developing their own software. The accounting requirements of many organisations are broadly similar, and so an application package can be developed which copes with most of them. (Some can be tailored to an organisation's specific requirements.) This also means that bugs or errors can be ironed out at an early stage.

PAPER 6
ELEMENTS OF INFORMATION SYSTEMS

Time allowed - 3 hours

Number of questions on paper - 7

Answer FIVE questions only

All questions carry equal marks

Candidates may use flowcharting templates

DO NOT OPEN THIS PAPER UNTIL YOU ARE READY TO START

UNDER EXAMINATION CONDITIONS

TEST PAPER: DECEMBER 1991 EXAMINATION

Answer FIVE questions only

1 Most users of small business computers need to purchase some type of printer for producing hard copy. These come in many different forms such as 'daisy wheel', 'dot matrix' and 'laserjet'. In addition to choice of type, selection also requires a level of technical understanding of terms such as 'parallel', 'serial' and 'interface'.

Required:

(a) Explain the difference between parallel and serial printers and clarify the meaning of the term interface. **(8 marks)**

(b) Briefly describe the *three* types of printer identified and explain their relative merits.
(12 marks)
(20 marks)

2 Pencils Plus Limited has 15 depots which supply stationery materials to retail shops. Their systems are computerised using a distributed network of five minicomputers which are regionally located.

Required:

(a) Define the term 'distributing data processing'. **(6 marks)**

(b) Briefly explain (with the aid of a diagram) how this company might organise its hardware to provide support to each depot. **(8 marks)**

(c) List the features of a typical minicomputer used in a distributed network. **(6 marks)**
(20 marks)

3 The power and flexibility of computers often makes them indispensable to an organisation. In these circumstances continuity of service is imperative so physical security and disaster planning are of vital importance to the users.

Required:

Identify five different physical risks to which a computer system is exposed, describe steps you would take to minimise these risks, and give details of recovery plans that you would prepare in the event of disaster. **(20 marks)**

4 FAAS plc has computerised its Fixed Assets Accounting System.

Required:

(a) Provide a screen layout for a file enquiry on a particular asset. **(6 marks)**

(b) Identify and explain the effects of *four* different transactions used to update the master file. **(8 marks)**

(c) Give *two* examples of information provided by such a system which would prove useful in effective operation of the business. **(6 marks)**
(20 marks)

5 Microcomputers are now available in many different styles for varying types of use.

Required:

Explain the main features and typical usage of the following types.

(a)	Desktop.	(5 marks)
(b)	Laptop.	(5 marks)
(c)	Hand held data collection device.	(5 marks)
(d)	Point of sale terminal.	(5 marks)
		(20 marks)

6 Information systems are implemented to produce useful information to improve the quality of decision making in organisations. Decisions need to be taken at operational, tactical and strategic levels by junior, middle and senior management staff.

Required:

At each of these *three* levels, in a system area of your choice, identify a typical decision which needs to be made, and give brief details of the information systems needed to support this decision.   (20 marks)

7 Explain the meaning of the following terms as they are used in a computing context.

(a)	Integrated package.	(4 marks)
(b)	User friendly.	(4 marks)
(c)	Local area network.	(4 marks)
(d)	Timesharing.	(4 marks)
(e)	Modem.	(4 marks)
		(20 marks)

TEST PAPER
SUGGESTED SOLUTIONS

DO NOT TURN THIS PAGE UNTIL YOU

HAVE COMPLETED THE TEST PAPER

1 (a) In general terms, an *interface* is the circuitry which connects two devices. Usually these two devices will be the central processor unit and a peripheral device, such as a printer. The interface receives signals from the CPU and converts these into signals that the peripheral can understand, and vice versa. Some interfaces are built into the computer's basic module, and some exist as free-standing units which require connection between the relevant devices.

An interface is most commonly used where signals need to be converted from series to parallel, or vice versa, and many modern computers have connecting 'ports' of both types.

A *parallel printer* is a printer which operates using signals received in parallel. This means that a signal, consisting of eight binary digits, is transmitted so that the eight bits travel side-by-side along eight separate wires simultaneously. This is the form of data transmission usually found in a computer.

A *serial printer* is a printer which uses signals received in series. This means that each of the 8 bits travel one after the other along a single wire. Each group of 8 bits, or byte, is then decoded by the printer. Because the printer has to wait until each group arrives before being able to decode the data, a serial printer is marginally slower than a parallel printer.

(b) A *daisy-wheel* printer uses technology developed from the traditional manual typewriter, but whereas in a traditional typewriter characters are embossed on keys which are set in rows, in a daisy-wheel printer the keys project outwards from a central hub. The keys give the appearance of petals on a flower, hence daisy-wheel.

Daisy-wheels are usually removable so that they can be replaced with a wheel containing a different font or type size. Again as with a traditional typewriter a character is printed by means of the relevant key being pressed against the printer's inked ribbon so that the imprint of the embossed letter appears on the page. The wheel must be rotated so that the relevant key is in the printing position. The spinning of the wheel is a constraint to fast printing - clearly only one character can be printed at a time and speed of printing may be up to about 80 characters per second.

A *dot-matrix* printer has a print head consisting of a grid of steel pins or needles. When a character is selected, a pre-set combination of pins is depressed, against a print ribbon, so that the character appears as a matrix of small dots. Typical grids are 9×9 pins or 9×7 pins. This means that the quality of printed output is fairly low, as the dots are visible to the naked eye. Dot matrix printers print one character at a time, but are faster than daisy-wheel printers, offering speeds of 100-400 cps. On higher density grids, a wide range of character styles is possible.

A *laser* printer prints onto individual sheets of paper rather than onto continuous stationery. It uses laser technology to fix ink onto paper by means of a combination of heat and pressure, an electrical charge being used to form characters. Laser printers produce high quality output and are frequently used to print charts and graphs because the technology does not limit the user to pre-set characters only. Laser printers print a line at a time, scanning a page rather as a photocopier does, and can produce around 10 A4 pages per minute. They are very quiet in operation, the loudest noise coming from the electro-mechanical paper feed.

2 (a) *Distributed data processing*

Distributed data processing is a term defined by the National Computer Centre as a system in which there are several autonomous but interacting processors and/or data stores at different geographical locations linked over a communications network. Typically this would involve a central mainframe computer linked to a number of microcomputers operating as intelligent terminals.

There is some flexibility in such computer system design, but the key features of distributed processing are as follows.

(i)   Computers are distributed or spread over a wide geographical area.

(ii) A computer in the system can access the information files of other computers in the system.

(iii) The ability for computers within the system to process data 'jointly' or 'interactively'.

(iv) *Processing* is either carried out centrally or at dispersed locations.

(v)   *Files* are held either centrally or at local sites.

(vi) *Authority* is decentralised as processing can be autonomously performed by local computers under local management.

(b) Pencils Plus Limited may choose to set up one minicomputer as a central unit. This would then be linked to each of the other minicomputers using modems and telecommunications lines. The central minicomputer would therefore provide a function as a link between each of the branch machines, but would also operate as a branch computer in its own right. Each minicomputer would be sited in a depot and thus five depots would require only local terminals (shown as 'L' in the diagram). The other ten would be equipped with remote terminals ('R') providing communications links to the nearest depot with a minicomputer.

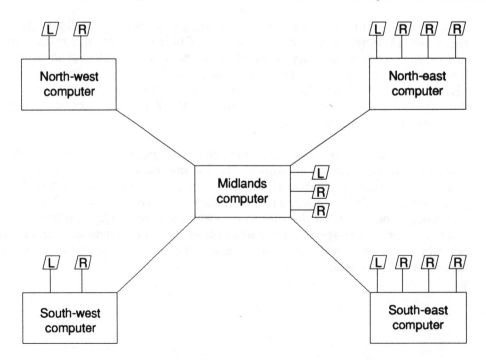

(c)   A typical minicomputer used in a distributed network would have the following features.

   (i)   They must be robust. They will be sited in a variety of locations (for example regional depots) and it is not possible to provide full mainframe-type facilities such as air-conditioning and a regulated power supply.

   (ii)   They must be compact. It is unlikely that some sites will offer the provision of a separate computer room and so they must fit unobtrusively into an office.

   (iii)   They must be easy to operate. Specialist staff will not be available except where major attention is required. Local operations staff must be able to use them.

   (iv)   They must be flexible. If it is desired to add terminals or other peripherals to a minicomputer, there must be capacity to allow this without seriously affecting the unit's performance.

   (v)   They must be able to communicate with the other minicomputers (or micros) in the network.

3   Physical security comprises two sorts of controls, protection against natural and man made disasters, such as fire, flood and sabotage, and protection against intruders gaining physical access to the system. These threats can be grouped alternatively as accidental and deliberate.

The physical environment has a major effect on information system security, and so planning it properly is an important precondition of an adequate security plan.

(a)   Fire is the most serious hazard to computer systems. Destruction of data can be even more costly than the destruction of hardware. A proper fire safety plan is an essential feature of security procedures, in order to prevent fire, detect fire and put out the fire. Fire safety includes:

   (i)   site preparation (eg appropriate building materials, fire doors);
   (ii)   detection (eg smoke detectors);
   (iii)   extinguishing (eg sprinklers);
   (iv)   training for staff in observing fire safety procedures (eg no smoking in computer room).

(b)   A proper environment must be provided for mainframes. Mainframe computers in particular are susceptible to damage from poor atmospheric or environmental conditions. A typical installation would provide air-conditioning, a dust-free environment (provided by use of special clothing and double sets of sealed doors), antistatic protection and 'clean' power supplies. Power supplies must be protected from both loss of power and irregularities in supply, both of which can corrupt data and processing activities.

(c)   Other natural disasters include flooding and abnormal weather conditions. It is difficult to envisage the form and effect of these, but certain steps can be taken. It may be unwise to site a computer in a basement, even if this is considered to be a more suitable location for machines than people, as this is likely to be the first area affected by flooding. Lightning may adversely affect power supplies.

(d)   The other main area of physical security is access control, to prevent intruders getting anywhere near the computer equipment or storage media. Methods of controlling human access include:

(i)   personnel (security guards);
(ii)   mechanical devices (eg keys, whose issue is recorded);
(iii) electronic identification devices (eg card-swipe systems, where a card is passed through a reader).

(e)   Theft is also a problem, particularly where so much computer equipment is easily portable. A microcomputer need not be larger than a briefcase and even a laser printer can be carried by one person. To some extent this can be guarded against by means similar to those described in (d), but with much equipment located in ordinary offices and no longer kept in a single secure location other measures must be taken. Regular 'stock controls' or physical inspections may be necessary, and a strictly imposed form of bookings used when staff take PCs off-site, either to customers or home.

One possible approach to disaster recovery is to use the services of a specialist disaster recovery company. These companies are becoming more widespread as computer users are made more aware of the potential dangers of a major disaster. These companies offer office premises with desks, telephones and storage space which are equipped with hardware, including terminals, of the same type as that used by their customers. In the event of a disaster, the customer can 'invoke' standby procedures and load backups of software to carry on essential business.

Disaster standby companies generally offer services to users of one hardware manufacturer's equipment only, and clearly require a number of subscribers if they are to offer a cost effective service. The upper limit on subscribers is governed by the probability that two customers require facilities at once; this is determined by insurers.

Alternatively, computer bureaux can agree to make their own systems available in the event of an emergency. Such an arrangement has to be specified in advance, as there might be other demands on a bureau's resources.

However, the key is to draw up a formal disaster recovery plan and to ensure maximum staff awareness of the appropriate procedures.

4   (a)   *Enquiry screen*

FIXED ASSETS ACCOUNTING SYSTEM
Enquiry off-line

Asset description ....

Asset no .... Date acquired ....
Location ....
Owner Department ....

Estimated useful life (months) ....
Serial no (manufacturer's) ....

Cost
Prior years' depreciation ....
Current year's depreciation ....
Book value (end of last period) ....

(b) *Transactions used to update the master file*

    (i) *Purchase of a fixed asset.* Whenever FAAS plc acquires an asset which meets its accounting requirements for capitalisation, this asset will be recorded in the fixed asset system. All relevant details of the item will be added to the master file.

    (ii) *Destruction of a fixed asset.* If any assets are destroyed or damaged beyond repair, they will need to be removed from the master file. Thus if a salesman writes off a company car, this should be deleted from the master file.

    (iii) *Physical shortfalls.* If during a fixed asset count, discrepancies are identified between physical and book, it will be necessary to decide to what extent these discrepancies should be reflected in the master file. Clearly full investigation of shortfalls together with suitable authorisation procedures should precede any update.

    (iv) *Transfer of assets.* Any transfer of assets between departments should be reflected in the master file to ensure that it is up to date. It is all too easy for assets such as motor vehicles, managed on a fleet basis, to be allocated to different departments, for example when a driver leaves or is given a new car. If depreciation charges are allocated to departments on the basis of assets 'owned', these will be misstated by reason of any failure to post transfers.

(c) *Effective operation of the business*

    (i) Details of an asset's location, manufacturer's serial number and company asset number will be required in the event of physical asset checks. FAAS plc should have its own procedures for physical checks (eg one department checked per quarter) and in any case the company's auditors will be likely to request details of specific assets for verification. A good system would be able to generate reports of assets owned by a particular department or located in a particular area/site.

    (ii) Details of fully written down assets will be useful in preparation of budgets. Decisions can be made on whether assets should be sold or need to be scrapped and when replacement should be planned. This is useful for setting the following year's capital expenditure budget and should be done anyway to ensure the system is purged of any fully written down items which are no longer in use.

5 (a) *Desktop*

A desktop computer is a small microcomputer which, as its name suggests, is usually located on a desk. This may be the desk of a user, rather than a separate position. Typically it will consist of a basic module (which includes floppy disk drives), a VDU on a pedestal and a keyboard. Several desktops will probably share a printer - they would not have one each. The VDU may be placed on the basic module 'box', or alternatively the box may be sited under or beside the desk. The VDU's pedestal allows it to be angled to suit the user.

A desktop enables easy access to a computer by regular users, and is extremely convenient.

(b) *Laptop*

A laptop is a small portable computer which can be sited on the user's lap or on a small work surface. It consists of a single unit incorporating processor, memory, hard disk, disk drive, keyboard and screen. The screen, which is of a flat design and usually with a liquid crystal or gas plasma display, is hinged and folds down to cover the keyboard, and is opened up for use. A typical laptop is around the size of a briefcase and has its own carrying handle. It has many uses including in meetings, on site visits, on train journeys and in hotels. It will run off the mains electricity supply but is also equipped with a rechargeable battery pack, which gives a couple of hours truly portable use per charge.

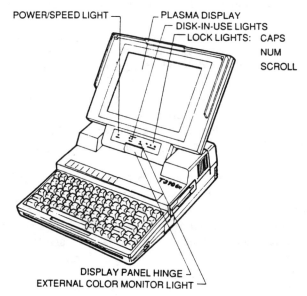

(c) *Hand held data collection device*

A hand held data collection device can take a number of forms. One application is in retail store stock control, where the device resembles a palm-sized pocket calculator. It is battery powered and on its face has a numeric keypad with certain special keys and a one or two line screen. Data is stored on suitable backing storage such as a microcassette. Data entry is either by means of the keypad or in combination with a linked device such as a bar-code reader. A stocktake can be effected by means of the user reading a product bar code (sited on the relevant shelf display) with the reader and then entering the quantity using the keypad. Data is then transferred via the tape to a computer and stocktake follow-up procedures can follow in the usual way with a comparison of book to actual.

(d) *Point of sale terminal*

More and more large retail stores are introducing electronic point of sale terminals which act both as cash registers and as terminals connected to a main computer. This enables the computer to produce useful management information such as sales details and analysis and stock control information very quickly. Many use bar coding or direct keyboard entry. A fully itemised, accurate and descriptive receipt can be produced for the customer, who will also feel the benefit of faster moving queues at the checkout. Management will obtain more information more quickly than was ever possible before, in particular:

(i)   immediate updating of book stock levels;
(ii)   identification of fast-moving items for reordering, hence avoidance of stock-outs;
(iii)   sales information.

The provision of immediate sales information (eg which products sell quickly), perhaps analysed on a branch basis, permits great speed and flexibility in decision-making (certainly of a short-term nature), as consumer wishes can be responded to quickly.

6 At the *operational* level management make decisions relating to the ongoing working of departments and individual sections of the organisation. Decisions at this level tend to be based on short-term considerations: the information required relates to factors concerned with the day-to-day operation and management of the organisation, such as whether machines are functioning correctly, whether customers who order are within their credit limits and what the overtime for the week has been. Managers use the information to monitor whether individual operations are being performed correctly.

At the *tactical* level management make decisions concerned with meeting the strategic objectives of the organisation, such as achieving budgets. Decisions are mainly based on medium term considerations, and the information required indicates the efficiency and effectiveness of the departments being managed, and how well they are meeting strategic objectives. In general management at the tactical level addresses neither specific day-to-day operations nor the setting of strategic objectives.

At the *strategic* level management make decisions concerned with long-term considerations and with setting objectives. In order to do so they will take into consideration information from both inside and outside the organisation. Company systems will produce the internal information while a number of different sources will provide the external information. The external sources used to supply information will differ according to how large the organisation is, the economic sector in which it operates and the type of activity in which it is engaged.

Take as an example a credit control operation in a large manufacturing company.

The credit controllers work at the operational level. The information they need relates to their being able to authorise the highest level of sales and collect the highest level of cash, while incurring the lowest cost in terms of bad and doubtful debts. They should also aim to minimise any loss of business which might arise from incorrectly placing good customers (or even customers who might have paid if supplies continued) on stop or hold. Decisions they make are aimed at achieving their objectives - high levels of authorised sales and cash collections and low levels of bad debts. The information which they need includes current figures relating to customers' recent purchases, payments and account status. They might also make use of external information on individual customers both from commercial sources (such as credit reference agencies) and from sources such as other suppliers and the media.

The credit control manager has the same overall objective as the controllers, but his focus shifts from being concerned about individual customers to wanting to ensure that budgetary and target figures for cash collected and bad debts fall within the targets he has agreed with his manager. Decisions he makes should be directed at trying to ensure that the targets are achieved. The information he needs would include summaries of activities at the operational level (giving, for example, total receipts, total credit notes issued, debts written off, totals of aged amounts outstanding and amounts outstanding where customers' credit limits or terms have been exceeded).

The financial director's focus shifts from looking at past performance to looking at the future. Decisions he makes relate to matters such as obtaining finance, placing funds on deposit and deciding between different investment strategies. The information he needs to do this comes both from summary reports from the credit control operation (eg how much is expected to be received this and next month, how much is currently outstanding, how that amount is likely to change based on previous trends in the business year, are any large customers in danger of collapsing in the near future, what proportion of the current debt is uninsured, what proportion is difficult to collect from overseas customers) as well as from outside sources such as the economic forecasts from various bodies, opinion polls regarding the expected stability of the government, expected movements in interest and exchange rates, information regarding difficult trading conditions in various sectors of the market which might indicate an increase in bad debts and information regarding firm trading conditions which might indicate expansion of credit requirements.

7 (a) *Integrated package*

There are two categories of package in common use. Packages may be general purpose, eg spreadsheets or word-processing, or they may be accounting packages, eg sales ledger or payroll. An integrated package consists of two or more individual packages which have been integrated so as to provide certain linking features. Thus an integrated accounting package may consist of a nominal ledger, sales ledger, purchase ledger and payroll. When a subsidiary ledger is updated, postings can be made directly to the nominal ledger without the need for data to be re-input. Similarly an integrated spreadsheet, word processing and database package makes it possible to import data direct to a spreadsheet from a database without the need to key it in first, and then to incorporate the results of spreadsheet work into a text under preparation.

(b) *User friendly*

This is a general term used to denote computer hardware or software which can be successfully operated by the inexperienced user. In the past, computers could only be operated and understood by experts, but with the widespread use of PCs by non-experts for the purpose of carrying on their own tasks (accounting, sales etc) it is necessary that these users can achieve results without having to resort to technical back-up for everything they do. One particular strategy to increase user-friendliness which is growing in popularity is WIMP. WIMP involves the use of two design ideas and two operating methods.

(i) *Windows*. This basically means that the screen can be divided into sections, 'windows' of flexible size which can be opened and closed. This enables two or more documents to be viewed and edited together, and sections of one to be inserted into another.

(ii) *Icons*. An icon is an image of an object used to represent an abstract idea or process. In software design, icons may be used instead of numbers, letters or words to identify and describe the various functions available for selection, or files to access. A common icon is a waste paper bin to indicate the deletion of a document.

(iii) *Mouse*. A mouse is a small device which sits on the desk, and is plugged into the basic module of the micro, or into the keyboard. Underneath the mouse is a hard ball. The mouse is rolled by hand across the desk top, and as the mouse moves around on the desktop a pointer (cursor) on the VDU screen mimics its movements. A mouse can be used to pick out the appropriate icon (or other option), to mark out the area of a new window, mark the beginning and end of a block for deletion/insertion etc. It also has a button to execute the current command. This is seen as more user-friendly than the combination of arrow keys and return key on a keyboard.

(iv) *Pull-down menu*. An initial menu (or 'menu-bar') will be shown across the top of the VDU screen. Using the mouse to move the pointer to the required item in the menu is somewhat similar to pulling down a window blind in the room of a house. The pointer and mouse can then be used to select the required item on the pulled-down menu.

(c) *Local area network*

A *local area network* (LAN) is a means of interconnecting a number of microcomputers over a small area (typically within a few hundred metres). Several sorts of networks exist, giving a variety of speed/cost/capacity trade-offs; essentially the faster the data transfer around the network, the more expensive the system. Basically the system consists of (i) a central disk file and program store, controlled by a dedicated microcomputer, and (ii) a cable or 'data highway' linking this control microcomputer to the other microcomputers. (The system works in a similar fashion to a ring main circuit for domestic electricity supply.)

A LAN is usually restricted to a single office or site - connections to other sites are by means of a WAN, which requires telecommunications lines to link sites.

(d) *Timesharing*

The concept of timesharing exists because a computer can process data many times faster than a human operator or user can give instructions for manipulation of data or input data. Each user has the impression that he has an immediate response from the computer and that there are no constraints on this use. Each user has his own terminal, consisting of a screen and keyboard; he may be remote from the processor. The computer divides its processor time into chunks and switches between users so quickly that no user is aware that any other users are also logged on to the processor.

(e) *Modem*

One of the problems with data transmission is that computer equipment stores and uses data in discrete digital (or 'bit') form, but data is sent along a telephone wire in a different form altogether - ie in wave form/analogue signals. For data transmission through the telephone network to be possible, it is necessary for there to be a device at each end of the telephone line which can convert the data signals in digital form to analogue form, and from analogue to digital form, depending on whether the data is being sent out or received along the telephone line. The equipment for converting data in this manner is called a modem (modulator/demodulator). It therefore provides an interface between the terminal equipment and the transmission line.

AAT PAPER 6 - ELEMENTS OF INFORMATION SYSTEMS

FURTHER READING

You may like to test your grasp of the subject by tackling short questions in multiple choice format. BPP publish the *Password* series of books, each of which incorporates a large collection of multiple choice questions with solutions, comments and marking guides. The *Password* title relevant to Elements of Information Systems is *Information Technology*. It is priced at £6.95 and contains about 350 questions.

To order your book, ring our credit card hotline on 081-740 6808 or tear out this page and send it to our Freepost address.

To: BPP Publishing Ltd, FREEPOST, London W12 8BR   Tel: 081-740 6808

Forenames (Mr / Ms): _____

Surname: _____

Address: _____

_____

Post code: _____

Please send me the following books:	*Quantity*	*Price*	*Total*
Password: Information Technology		£6.95	

Please include postage:

UK: £1.50 for first plus £0.50 for each extra book   ....

Overseas: £3.00 for first plus £1.50 for each extra book   ....

I enclose a cheque for £_____ or charge to Access/Visa

Card number ☐☐☐☐☐☐☐☐☐☐☐☐☐☐☐☐☐☐

Expiry date _____ Signature _____

If you are placing an order, you might like to look at the reverse of this page. It's a Review Form, which you can send in to us with comments and suggestions on the kit you've just finished. Your feedback really does make a difference: it helps us to make the next edition that bit better. So if you're posting the coupon, do fill in the Review Form as well.

AAT PAPER 6 – ELEMENTS OF INFORMATION SYSTEMS

Name: _____

How have you used this kit?

Home study (book only) ☐ With 'correspondence' package ☐

On a course: college_____ ☐ Other _____

How did you obtain this kit?

From us by mail order ☐ From us by phone ☐

From a bookshop ☐ From your college ☐

Where did you hear about BPP kits?

At bookshop ☐ Recommended by lecturer ☐

Recommended by friend ☐ Mailshot from BPP ☐

Advertisement in _____ ☐ Other _____

Have you used the companion text for this subject?   Yes/No

Your comments and suggestions would be appreciated on the following areas.

Study guide and quiz

Content of solutions

Errors (please specify, and refer to a page number)

Presentation

Other